LESSONS IN ART

BY

HUME NISBET

AUTHOR OF

'LIFE AND NATURE STUDIES' 'THE PRACTICAL IN PAINTING' ETC.

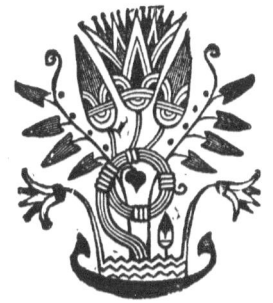

British Library Cataloguing-in-Publication Data
A catalogue record for this book is available from
the British Library

Drawing and Illustration

Drawing is a form of visual art that can make use of any number of drawing instruments, including graphite pencils, pen and ink, inked brushes, wax colour pencils, crayons, charcoal, chalk, pastels and various kinds of erasers, markers, styluses, metals (such as silverpoint) and even electronic drawing. As a medium, it has been one of the most popular and fundamental means of public expression throughout human history – as one of the simplest and most efficient means of communicating visual ideas.

Drawing itself long predates other forms of human communication, with evidence for its existence preceding that of the written word – demonstrated in cave paintings of around 40,000 years ago. These drawings, known as pictograms, depicted objects and abstract concepts including animals, human hands and generalised patterns. Over time, these sketches and paintings were stylised and simplified, leading to the development of the written language as we know it today. This form of drawing can truly be considered art in its purest sense – the basic forms on which all others build.

Whilst the term 'to draw' derives from the Old English *dragan* (meaning 'to drag, draw or protract'), the word 'illustrate' derives from the Latin word *illustratio,* meaning 'enlighten' or 'irradiate'. This process of 'enlightenment' is central to drawing and illustration as we know it today. Medieval codices' illustrations were often called 'illuminations', designed to highlight and further explain important aspects of biblical texts. This was the most general form of illustration; hand-created, individual and unique. This changed in the fifteenth century however, when books began to be illustrated with woodcuts – most notably in Germany, by Albrecht Dürer.

The first creative impulses of a painter or sculptor are commonly expressed in drawings, and architects and photographers are commonly trained to draw, if for no other reason than to train their perceptual skills and develop their creative potential. Initially, artists used and re-used wooden tablets for the production of their drawings, however following the widespread availability of paper in the fourteenth century, the use of drawing in the arts increased. During the Renaissance (a period of massive flourishing of human intellectual endeavours and creativity), drawings exhibiting realistic and representational qualities emerged. Notable draftsmen included Leonardo da Vinci, Michelangelo and Raphael. They were inspired by the concurrent developments in geometry and philosophy, exhibiting a true synthesis of these branches – a combination somewhat lost in the modern day.

Figure drawing became a recognised subsection of artistic drawing in this period, despite its long history stretching back to prehistoric descriptions. An anecdote by the Roman author and philosopher Pliny, describes how Zeuxis (a painter who flourished during the 5th century BCE) reviewed the young women of Agrigentum naked before selecting five whose features he would combine in order to paint an ideal image. The use of nude models in the medieval artist's workshop is further implied in the writings of Cennino Cennini (an Italian painter), and a manuscript of Villard de Honnecourt confirms that sketching from life was an established practice by the thirteenth century. The Carracci, who opened their *Accademia degli Incamminati* (one of the first art academies in Italy) in Bologna in the 1580s, set the pattern for later art schools by making life drawing the central discipline. The course of training began with the copying of engravings, then proceeded to drawing from plaster casts, after which the students were trained in drawing from the live model.

The main processes for reproduction of drawings and illustrations in the sixteenth and seventeenth centuries were engraving and etching, and by the end of the eighteenth century, lithography (a method of printing originally based on the immiscibility of oil and water) allowed even better illustrations to be reproduced. In the later seventeenth and eighteenth centuries, the previous combination of the arts and sciences in drawing gave way to a more romantic and even classical style, epitomised by draftsmen such as Poussin, Rembrandt, Rubens, Tiepolo and Antoine Watteau. Mastery in drawing was considered a prerequisite to painting, and students in Jacques-Louis David's Studio (a famed eighteenth century French painter of the neo-classical style), were required to draw for six hours a day, from a model who remained in the same pose for an entire week!

During this period, an increasingly large gap started to emerge between 'fine artists' on the one hand, and 'draftsmen' / 'illustrators' on the other. This difference became further complicated with the 'Golden Age of Illustration'; a period customarily defined as lasting from the latter quarter of the nineteenth century until just after the First World War. In this period of no more than fifty years the popularity, abundance and most importantly the unprecedented upsurge in quality of illustrated works marked an astounding change in the way that publishers, artists and the general public came to view artistic drawing. Arthur Rackham, Walter Crane, John Tenniel and William Blake are some of its most famous names. Until the latter part of the nineteenth century, the work of illustrators was largely proffered anonymously, and in England it was only after Thomas Bewick's pioneering technical advances in wood engraving that it became common to acknowledge the artistic and technical expertise of illustrators. Such draftsmen also frequently used their drawings in preparation for paintings, further obfuscating the distinction between drawing/painting, high/low art.

The artists involved in the Arts and Crafts Movement (with a strong emphasis on stylised drawing, and a powerful influence on the 'Golden Age of Illustration') also attempted to counter the ever intruding Industrial Revolution, by bringing the values of beautiful and inventive craftsmanship back into the sphere of everyday life. This helped to counter the main challenge which emerged around this time – photography. The invention of the first widely available form of photography (with flexible photographic film role marketed in 1885) led to a shift in the use of drawing in the arts. This new technology took over from drawing as a superior method of accurately representing the visual world, and many artists abandoned their painstaking drawing practices. As a result of these developments however, modernism in the arts emerged – encouraging 'imaginative originality' in drawing and abstract formulations. Drawing was once again at the forefront of the arts.

There are many different categories of drawing, including figure drawing, cartooning, doodling and shading. There are also many drawing methods, such as line drawing, stippling, shading, hatching, crosshatching, creating textures and tracing – and the artist must be aware of complex problems such as form, proportion and perspective (portrayed in either linear methods, or depth through tone and texture). Today, there are also many computer-aided drawing tools, which are utilised in design, architecture, engineering, as well as the fine arts. It is often exploratory, with considerable emphasis on observation, problem-solving and composition, and as such, remains an unceasingly useful tool in the artists repertoire.

The processes of drawing is a fascinating artistic practice, enabling a beautiful array of effects and creative expression. As is evident from this short introduction, it also has an incredibly old history, moving from decorations on cave walls to the most advanced, realistic and imaginative drawings possible in the present day. It is hoped that the current reader enjoys this book on the subject.

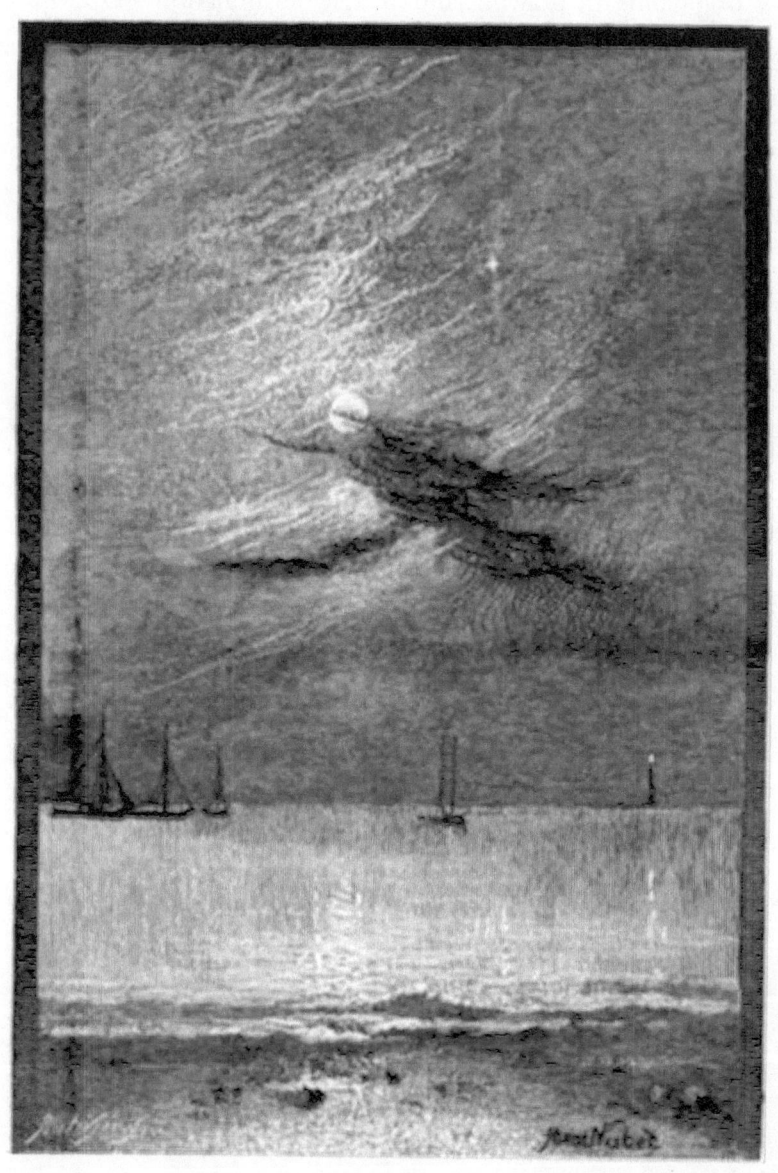

THE RISING MOON

LIFE AND NATURE STUDIES.

By HUME NISBET.

WITH ETCHING BY C. O. MURRAY, AND ILLUSTRATIONS
BY THE AUTHOR.

Professor John Ruskin, LL.D. :—' A real faculty for colour and
sensibility to beauty. I have great hope that your gift for colour
will make you an extremely popular, prosperous, and in a true
sense excellent artist.'

The Athenæum :—' Inspired with much sympathy for his subject, and
guided by native good taste.'

The Spectator :—'Bright and chatty, with an intense love of colour,
and a touch of the didactic sufficient to impress them on the art
student. The illustrations are delicate and possess plenty of the
freedom and nervousness of outline which he urges so strongly.'

Atalanta :—' Mr. Nisbet has many of the combined attributes of painter
and poet. His book is partly practical, but it surprises one also
with quaint and fascinating thoughts, sometimes deep, sometimes
subtile, and always beautiful.'

The Publishers' Circular :—' Contains the largest amount of information in the smallest possible space, and is withal endowed with the
spirit of poetry.'

The Bookseller :—' Contains much useful information.'

The Morning Post :—' Marked by a feeling of intense love of Nature,
and a clear insight into art.'

The Daily Review :—'Close observation and keen appreciation of
Nature.'

The Scotsman :— ' The unconventional mode of their expression gives
a certain freshness to the doctrines of the writer.

The Scottish News :—' Mr. Nisbet is a man who thinks for himself on all subjects ; he has, moreover, in a remarkably high degree, the power of expressing his ideas in a vigorous and unconventional manner.'

Dundee Advertiser :—' His remarks invariably show exact observation.'

Glasgow Herald :—' Daring originality.'

Stirling Observer :—' Strong individuality.'

Border Record :—' A work of many and strong claims on the attention of artists and general readers.'

The Border Advertiser :—' Treated in a way that is at once striking and fascinating.'

Newcastle Daily Leader :—' Technical knowledge interwoven with the dexterity and skill of a master.'

Newcastle Weekly Chronicle :—' A book to caress and linger over. Of great practical, value. The reading and studying will produce a reverence alike for the subject and the author.'

The Kelso Chronicle :—' There is much of sober and wise instruction for the student.'

The Western Antiquary :—' It is a treat to handle such a book as this, and a greater treat still to peruse it. He has the observing eye, the poetic imagination, and the versatile powers.'

The League Journal :—' It conveys many sound lessons.'

The Christian Leader :—' An artistic and literary Ishmaelite of the right sort.'

The People's Friend :—' Mr. Nisbet is himself an artist, and he writes like a poet on his art.'

The Chiel :—' Remarkable work of this painter, poet, novelist, and altogether extraordinary man. Steadily he has made his way into the hearts of those who love art for art's sake.'

Dunfermline Press :—' At times he rises to a remarkable height of descriptive powers.'

Ouida :—' Vigorous and original writings.'

Rev. W. Pulsford :—' Soul pulse through the type.'

Sir Noel Paton, LL.D., R.S.A. :—' Delicate and vivid word pictures.'

Dedicated

WITH HOPEFUL WISHES FOR THEIR FUTURE SUCCESS

TO MY TWO NEAREST PUPILS

MADGE HENRIETTA
AND
JOCELYN GEORGE NISBET

PREFACE

I HAVE endeavoured to write out in the following pages some of the strictly necessary rules and Laws of Drawing and Painting for the use of students, so that they may be able to work at home, and spare their masters a number of questions if they are at Art Schools.

Having had eight years' experience as art master of the Old School of Arts, Edinburgh, during the long interval between two travelling tours abroad, I had leisure to think the matter carefully out, and know to some extent what students are likely to ask, and want to learn, besides knowing what they ought to learn in their different stages.

I have looked back to my own student days, and tried to explain concisely those things which troubled me mostly then. I have also remembered the daily questions which I was forced to answer to each fresh pupil during those pleasant if not over-exciting eight years of my experience as an artist and art teacher; and I think that I have answered most of them as conscientiously and as plainly as it is possible to reply to such problems, and also as I always tried to answer and solve any questions in that past, without mystery or evasion.

In my art classes I used to have a considerable number of grown-up ladies and gentlemen who, having in some cases gone through other Art Schools, came to get a few finishing touches from me as an artist in my own particular line. At their request I wrote my book, 'Life and Nature Studies,' which I am glad to see has been utilised a good deal since its first appearance; and as its intention was to do good to art and artists, I rest satisfied in this result.

But while writing that book for the grown-up and partly experienced readers, I quite forgot my young students, and their wants. Therefore I now try to make up for that mistake, and trust that this present manual may help them along from the first stroke until they are ready for the more extensive flights and intricacies of 'Life and Nature Studies.'

H. N.

HOGARTH CLUB,
36 DOVER STREET, PICCADILLY, W.

CONTENTS

PART FIRST

DRAWING

PART SECOND

PAINTING IN WATER AND OIL COLOUR

PART THIRD

HINTS ON GENERAL ART

LIST OF ILLUSTRATIONS

LESSONS IN ART

PART FIRST

DRAWING

CHAPTER I

DRAWING MATERIALS

THERE is only one perfect way of learning Art, as any other profession or accomplishment, and that is, to begin at the very beginning ; think nothing too unimportant, and, above all, never grow impatient, no matter how slowly you seem to be getting on.

The beginning of painting is the art of drawing, and the beginning of drawing is the choosing rightly your materials, therefore I will begin with that very important preliminary.

Pencils, a sharp pen-knife, indiarubber, paper, drawing board and drawing pins. These have to be carefully considered if you wish to avoid a

B

number of unnecessary vexations; the *necessary* humiliations and obstacles which start up from the very Alpha to the Omega of art I do not wish you to avoid, but rather to meet them bravely and patiently, and so transform them into lasting pleasures.

Get a good HB pencil to begin with—the very best HB that is manufactured is the pencil you ought to have—and as you only require this one pencil for the present, be sure that you have the best.

Be particular also about your indiarubber and paper; if you do not know good indiarubber when you see and feel it, get some friend who has a knowledge of it to select a cake for you. India-rubber which is flexible and bends easily is generally the best for rubbing out, as it will not wear away the paper too much; try several pieces with your fingers, and decide upon the biggest, thickest and most easily bending cake, for if it is a proper piece you will grow very fond of it, and wish it to last as long as possible, so that the bigger it is, the better it will be for your purpose.

The paper is a thing of great importance; for the drawing which you have to do first, cartridge is good enough, only see that you get the very best and thickest cartridge paper, of medium roughness and firm surface. By this precaution you gain a great deal more than you might think, because your indiarubber will not wear holes in it, so that you will have time to complete your drawing ; also, as you have to pay more for your paper, you will not be in such a hurry to be finished with it, therefore you will be able to learn something from each sheet of paper, instead of doing a lot of useless work.

Bear always in mind that your preliminary work is of no value as drawings, it has only to be valued for the good it is doing to your eye and your hand, therefore be sure that you understand your shortcomings before you give up that sheet of paper, or pin a fresh sheet on your drawing board.

The best board for your purpose is the size that will hold half a sheet of paper ; divide the sheet in two parts, but only pin one half down at a time, and be careful to see that your drawing board is perfectly free from dust, grit, or scratches, so that you may have comfort in your work.

Use only large drawing pins, with strong points and massive heads, so that they may be easily taken out. Until you have learned outline drawing thoroughly, you will not require any other materials.

CHAPTER II

PERPENDICULAR, HORIZONTAL, AND SLANTING LINES

As in penmanship, your first subject to copy should be straight horizontal, slanting, and perpendicular, lines, as these form the basis of all drawing.

Do not attempt to produce many lines ; three parallel lines in each direction will be quite enough

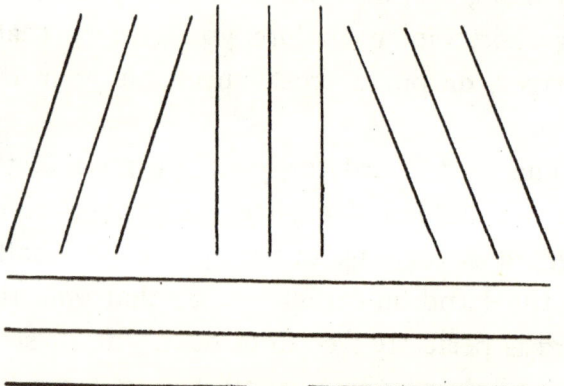

FIG. I—STRAIGHT AND SLANTING LINES

to educate you, if you pay particular attention to your work.

Place your copy in front of your board so that you can see it easily, and after studying the lines carefully, begin from the top, very lightly and slowly at first, and bring your pencil down to the end without lifting it from the paper, then choose the distance of your spaces between the lines and try to keep them as equal as possible. Draw three perpendicular lines lightly, as long lines as you can make, and then study them carefully before you begin to correct them.

Of course, they will be very uneven at the first ; you do not require a teacher to tell you this, or point out where the faults lie, which with a little attention you can see for yourselves.

There are two or three ways of sharpening a pencil. Professor John Ruskin is strong upon what he calls the level point. For preliminary work be particular not to cut away the wood too much ; make it taper up gradually from the cut to the lead and with square sides, the fewer the better, bringing the lead up to a long point, but not too sharp —a nice soft point is best.

Do not hurry over these three lines which you have drawn, or think that you are getting on by covering your paper with parallel lines. If you persevere at those three lines until they are straight, and at equal distances from each other, you have completed your lesson, and may go in for something more elaborate without loss of time. Three perpendicular, three horizontal, three slanting lines from right to left, and three from left to right, and if you are very careful, you need do no more of them, as you will be constantly coming upon them in your after work.

Make all your lines of equal length, i.e., the horizontal and slanting, as long as your perpendicular ones. In order to do this properly measure your spaces of paper, before beginning, with your eyes only ; afterwards you may satisfy yourself, if you like, by measuring with your pencil, only draw in the lines lightly before you do this, and depend mostly upon your eyes : remember that when you come before Nature you will have to depend altogether upon your eyes, so that it is your duty to educate those members from the beginning, and then you will be able to depend upon them when you want them most.

I have no wish to keep you a moment longer on copies than I can help ; I want to get you and myself out to the open air with our models before us, when we may be producing work of some pecuniary value ; therefore pay great attention to all that I say now, and have done with it as soon as possible.

Of course, I should advise any one whose ambition begins and ends with certificates and diplomas, to enter the ordinary Art Schools, and, while there, to conform strictly to their rules and regulations; by doing this, he will get what he desires.

The great advantages of these schools are the qualities of patience and correctness which they teach ; these are two of the big lessons in life that a youthful artist has to acquire.

When you have drawn your three faulty lines out lightly, look at them and the spaces between, and put the shaky parts right with touches and by degrees, rubbing out with your indiarubber the mistakes. Rub softly and patiently, and thus you will not wear either paper or rubber too much ; and then, when you are fairly satisfied that your lines are straight and your distances equal, go over them again and again from top to bottom with your pencil, so that each line when finished will be full of feeling and softness, and in a single line you will have twenty or more—all practice for your hand and eyes. Do the same with your horizontal and slanting lines, studying them and the perpendiculars as you proceed, so that when you have filled up your first sheet you will have learnt three great lessons, besides the drawing of straight lines :—(1) Control and judgment ; (2) The first principles of composition and design, and (3) The value and tenderness of a black lead pencil, for you will have learnt that a black line is not made by one decided, heavy mark, but by the repeated passing over lightly with your point.

CHAPTER III

CURVES

IF your paper bears the impress of your design on the reverse side, then you have hurried over and spoilt your work.

A good artistic line ought to be laid on to the surface of the paper with the lightness and delicacy of a floating feather, and never penetrate or *impress* the paper. The moment that the indiarubber will not remove it easily, or, when it is removed, leaves behind an indented mark, then be sure that you have spoilt your sheet; cast it aside and begin a new one, only do not let that occur more than once in your lifetime; an unfinished sheet of paper is one step backwards: always go forward, never backward.

Darkness is not blackness; if you press your pencil down heavily you will cut into the paper, produce blackness and make an ungainly hard line; if you go over the first faint line often, you will produce darkness, make a line full of colour and delicate firmness, and while you are doing this you will be learning the true art of shading.

Let us consider that you have now finished your first half-sheet and mastered the principles of straight lines; it may have taken you three or four nights, it ought not to have taken you less than two nights, to get through this task. If you have laboured conscientiously for four or even six nights over this simple study, then you have learnt something which you will never forget, and which will be extremely interesting and useful to you in the future.

One great point I wish to impress upon you, and that is, do not try to hurry over your first study.

We now come to the drawing of curved lines, half and quarter circles, which represent the embellishment of leaves, flowers, ornament, and the human figure, etc. This study is required so that it may give you a free and flowing hand, and the best way to succeed in the first sketching of it is to imagine your hand to be a pair of compasses, with the little finger as the resting prong, and the rest of the hand held easy and from the paper.

You will always draw a circle or half-circle best if you hold your pencil loosely, between the thumb, first and second fingers, and as far from the point as you can, that is, a long pencil is better than a short one for this practice.

Begin the curved, serpentine line with your centre straight line (see fig. 2), make a slight dot in the exact centre of the line, and then begin your curve from the top and do not stop until you have finished it, after this study it over once more, and correct it in parts, until you have it exactly, after

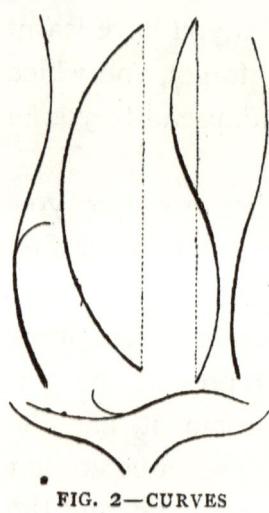

FIG. 2—CURVES

which go over the line slightly and often, until you have gained confidence enough to draw one easily. As a rule, curves are much more easily drawn with a little practice than are straight lines, only that they require constant practice to do them easily; they represent the scales in piano practice, and are very good for the wrist and fingers, only in general drawing it is the square lines which impart firmness and power to all subjects whether elaborate or otherwise.

CHAPTER IV

ORNAMENTAL DRAWING

IN the lines which Nature gives to us throughout a single leaf, you have all and more than can be got out of the most elaborate frieze or *bas-relief*; yet, as I do not expect that you will be far enough advanced to be able to grasp the intricacies and subtleties of a leaf, I can only advise you to get hold of some of the copper-plate ornamental designs which all Art Schools provide, and educational publishers bring out as first-grade studies.

Not too many of them though, for although you cannot be too exact in your imitation of objects before you, I do not wish you to become enslaved or formal in your imitation ; the copies which you are drawing from have nearly all been taken from the ancient Greek designs, and were originally taken direct from flowers and leaves.

Begin with the design most free from elaboration and detail, where two sides balance equally. It is only a continuation of the straight and curved lines which you have already drawn. Begin with the centre line, boxing in the others with slanting and square lines which will make you sure in your proportions. After you are satisfied with this part of the design, proceed to fill it in with the curved sides, drawing each corresponding line after you have done its fellow, and so on until your ornament is all sketched in.

Always sketch your subject completely but very faintly, in all its proportions, unless it is an elaborate subject, in which case you will pass a line outside of where your details come in, only designing the masses *as squarely* as you possible can do. (See fig. 3.)

Make a selection from the copybook of ornaments which you have bought, passing over two perhaps after the first, and taking the fourth

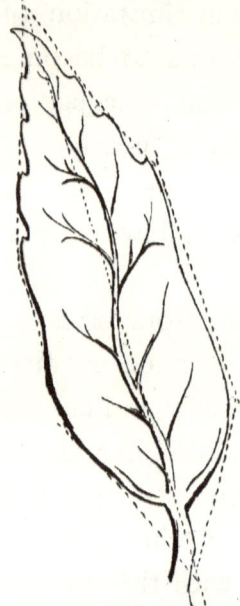

subject, after that the sixth, or whatever interests you most, and presents something decidedly different from the last copy which you have drawn, and after boxing or blocking it all with square lines, get gradually into the details, and do not leave it until you feel quite satisfied that it is like your copy and that you have missed no point.

It is better practice to make your copy larger than the original, if your example is small. Arrange your drawing at the commencement so that your half-

FIG. 3—STUDY OF A LEAF

sheet will hold it easily, leaving a margin on all sides.

Begin all drawings with the foundation or centre line, perpendicular if upright, horizontal if oblong, then make cross lines where the principal points are supposed to stand, after this make squares round the outside of the subject so as to be sure of your spaces ; the rest is comparatively easy work if you take sufficient time over the first planning out, which is really the important part of all drawing.

Never begin a subject that you are not intensely interested with, and when you feel sure that you understand the motive which rules all ornament, curved and straight lines, do not waste any more time over elaborate studies ; for in the correct drawing of a single sweeping line you will have learned as much as in a hundred copies of ornate details ; they are only repetitions of the same line in a larger or smaller degree. You have now learnt to draw firmly and feelingly, and so had better tackle at once the Round, or from Nature.

CHAPTER V

DRAWING FROM NATURE

PICK a fresh, green leaf from the nearest tree or bush, and lay it lightly down on a sheet of paper, a little distance from you, and begin to apply the rules which your ornamental work has taught you to the outline drawing of this single leaf. (See fig 3.)

The centre line first, next the outside lines, and

afterwards the veins and curved irregularities : a leaf which looks the most perfectly plain will be the best to begin with ; as it is, you will not be able to find any leaf in Nature which has a perfectly straight line about it, or an outer edge free from delicate curvatures.

Next take a small branch with perhaps three or four leaves attached ; which lay down, plan out, and draw carefully as you have done the single leaf.

After this get hold of a bare branch, and set it up before you. (See fig. 4.) You will be astonished, as you study it carefully, what an amount of fine drawing there is about that simple twig, and how very beautiful it is in the intricacy and variety of its details and graceful gradations of taperings and twistings.

Your most elaborate ornamental drawing has been child's play compared with this twig ; do not leave it alone until you have mastered some of its mystery of detail, for in that twig you have got the key-note to all landscape painting.

Your next study in subtilty should be a shaft or stalk of grass. Pluck up one as near the root as you can, and set to work upon it while it is wavy and fresh ; make your copy larger than the original, and before you are half through with the planning out of those serpentine lines, you will think how blind you have been all your life to the exquisite loveliness of Nature, and what a

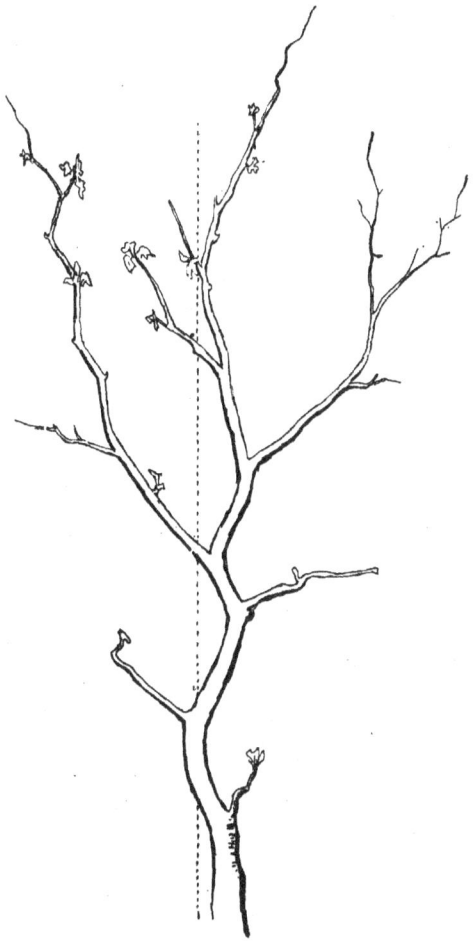

FIG. 4—STUDY OF A BRANCH

great power of enjoyment this new accomplishment is imparting to you, for I do not know of anything so graceful as a blade of grass.

After you have satisfactorily accomplished this study, you may look about you and select for yourselves the subjects you like best, perhaps a bunch of apple blossom, a lily, or a flower of any kind. Begin by taking a single bud, spray, or flower, and draw each until you understand all their curves and foldings ; then set up a group together and sketch them in mass, with the glass or cup in which you place them. Here you will encounter a new difficulty, viz., the art of making the cup appear standing and not falling over, which I shall now try to explain as simply as I can, as the same laws which govern that cup and table-top govern the drawing out of streets, houses, and landscapes in general.

CHAPTER VI

RULES OF PERSPECTIVE

WHEREVER you place your feet, whether it is in a room, or in the street, or in the middle of a field, becomes your standpoint, or the point where you stand.

Directly opposite your eyes, as you look straight out, and on a level with your eyes, whether you are standing, sitting, or lying, is your point of sight, or the centre point of your landscape.

An imaginary line passes from your eye to this point of distance, or point of sight, whichever you like to call it; this is called your first or centre line of distance, which is made straight out from you or perpendicularly from the standpoint, i.e. the bottom of your paper to the point of sight, let us say about half-way up the paper if you are standing while watching the scene.

Across the paper, and on a level with your point of sight, you draw a horizontal line, which represents the horizon. Only, of course, if you are looking over the sea from a height the real horizon may be beneath your eye, or if you are in a valley and lofty mountains in front, they may be above your eyes ; yet that does not matter : this is your horizontal line, which governs all the rest, because all objects above that line you look up to, objects below that line you look into or down upon.

So you have, as the nucleus of your landscape, the standpoint, point of sight or distance, perpendicular line of sight, and the horizontal level line.

From the point of distance spread out a number of imaginary lines, like the rays from a rising or setting sun, which spread in slanting lines on every side of that point, above, below, to right or left, until they fill up your entire piece of paper as they

C

do the landscape; these are the lines of direction or vanishing lines, because they all vanish into that point of distance or sight.

Whatever object in the scene meets your eye comes within the range of some of these vanishing lines; if above the horizontal line, then, as they become more distant, they will grow less and approach that point in a downward direction; if below

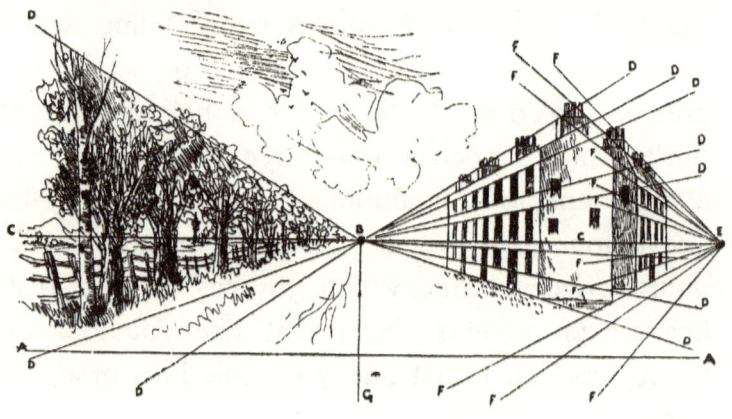

FIG. 5—A STUDY IN PERSPECTIVE

A. Standpoint.   B. Point of sight.   C. Horizontal line.   D. Vanishing lines.
E. Point of distance.   F. Vanishing lines of distance.   G. Line of sight.

that line, then they will grow less or recede by coming up to it.

For instance, an avenue of trees or a terrace of houses stand from you, growing less as they get distant.

Your horizontal line passes through very nearly

a third of the height of the houses or trees nearest to you, leaving the tops of the trees and roofs of the houses above, and the roots of the trees and basements of houses below the horizontal line.

If you draw a number of spreading rays or lines from your point of distance to the extremities of trees and houses on both sides nearest to you, or hold up your walking-stick where they are supposed to be, and look past it with one eye shut, you will be able to see at once that all the houses and trees keep within those lines, while it is the same with all your windows and doors etc.—they slant upwards when above the horizontal level line in a lesser or greater degree as they stand near or far from that level line, and downwards when they are below it.

You now comprehend the use of your vanishing lines in drawing, and how impossible it is to get along without them.

These are the simpler rules which must govern all objects above or below the horizontal line.

If you have placed the top of the cup which contains the flower you wish to draw on a level with the horizontal line, i.e. directly the same height as your eyes where you are sitting, then you will not be able to see the inside at all ; the round top will not appear anything else than a straight horizontal line.

In such a case, however, the bottom of the cup must necessarily be below the horizontal line where you look down upon it; therefore you will see that the lowest point is the centre of the bottom rim with the curved line receding on *both sides* towards the horizontal line,—which brings us to another law in perspective.

Let us suppose that the cup has been placed a little to one side of the point of sight. If it had been placed directly against it, you would see both sides equally; as it is, you will see most of the side which lies next to the line and point of sight, and just a little of the other.

Now, in order to be able to see the farther side of that cup, you must take your eyes away from the point of sight and look past the extreme edge to another point on the horizontal line, which forces you to turn towards the side of the picture, and again fix upon another point of distance ; these secondary or accidental points can only be determined by the object you are looking at, and when it stands from the main centre point of sight ; if it is a square block, the bottom line will guide your eye better than any other portion.

Watch how it stands off and where the line meets the horizontal, for that will be your extreme *oblique* point of distance ; it is termed the oblique point because, as you face your centre, you have to turn, or glance obliquely in order to get to it.

That oblique point of distance will govern all you can see of the side farthest from you ; as the object nears the horizon, the slanting lines will be more horizontal ; as it goes from it, they will be more perpendicular.

Thus, to take the cup. The side facing the perpendicular line and point of sight will recede towards the point on the line which passes from the centre of the bottom rim towards the direct point of sight, and all rings, etc., which may go round it will recede by thinner or more oval rings as they near the horizontal line.

The side farthest from you must be governed exactly the same by the oblique point of distance and the line or ray that touches the centre of the bottom rim and crosses the oblique point of distance.

This oblique lower ray must meet the direct ray from the point of sight a little way below the cup where it stands, because it has its sharp corner rounded off; but if it were a box or a house, with its edge turned towards you, then the true and false lines would meet at the nearest corner.

This is the principle of what is termed angular perspective,—which continually appeals to us in

our sketching from nature, and is apt to trouble
and perplex us in the multiplicity of objects that
may be scattered about, such as chairs, tables,
stools, boxes, ornaments in all directions and positions, outside or in, and which yet are perfectly
simple to grasp and arrange correctly, if we only
reduce the whole matter to first principles, and do
not allow ourselves to become confused, and so
lose our grip of the subject. Thus every object,
no matter what its position may be, must be
governed by those fixed laws of perspective—
firstly, the standpoint; secondly, the point of sight;
thirdly, the line of distance; fourthly, the horizontal
line; and fifthly, the direct vanishing lines; these
are the fixed laws which nothing can alter. (See
fig. 5.)

Every side of an object which presents its surface toward the perpendicular line of sight, either
to right or left, slants directly towards the point of
sight.

All surfaces or undersides which lie below or
above the horizontal line, are determined in their
width by the acuteness or obtuseness of the slanting lines, aided, of course, in cases of angular
objects or objects presenting sharp corners to the
spectator, by the corresponding oblique slanting
lines of distance, which meet and cross the direct
slanting lines.

All sides that verge from the spectators by reason of the object being placed obliquely or angularly and away from the point of sight towards a point of distance, whether it be to the left or right of the centre, incline in acuter or obtuser lines towards this second or accidental point, which, as I have said, is determined by the angle of the object itself, instead of by the spectator, as in the case of the fixed point of sight.

To get this angle correctly you must draw an imaginary line from the point nearest to you on the object to the horizon, and let all the other rays verge from that.

Thus in a drawing you can only have one point of sight, one real horizontal line, and one perpendicular line ; but you may have any number of accidental points of distance, according to the number and position of objects lying about, yet you must not have more than one accidental point of distance to each object.

There are also some cases (not often) when the necessity arises to make false horizontal lines, above or below the real horizontal line, as in the case of some tumble-down houses built eccentrically on slanting terraces and hillsides or valleys; but it is needless to trouble you with these intricacies. You have learnt enough to enable you, if you attend to it, to draw in correct positions any object which

may be placed before you. As we progress together, these laws of perspective and other laws
will come up and be explained in their proper
places.

CHAPTER VII

MEASURING TREE WORK, ETC.

WINTER time, early spring, or late autumn, when
the tree world is perfectly denuded of leafage, are
the best times for a young beginner to approach
Nature for the first time with sketch-book and
pencil.

Provide yourself for this purpose with a sketch-
ing-stool—one with a strong leather top is the
best and most comfortable--a sketch-block of
smooth paper, and two pencils, H and HB. The
sketch-block should not be less than ten or twelve
inches—larger, if possible.

Walk out with the express intention of finding
some object to interest you. Do not be over-am-
bitious at first, and you will not be disappointed
in the result; but be sure that you like the
object you fix upon better than anything else
about you, otherwise you may grow wearied of
it before you have seen a tenth part of its
beauties.

I may suggest that you decide upon the trunk of a birch or fir tree for your foreground, as in the copy which I have given you, with whatever else comes within range of your paper ; the object nearest you is what you must always concentrate your attention upon most.

Fix your seat, and sit down to look at it carefully and leisurely, studying each line and curve, so as to understand them and their relations to each other before ever you put your pencil to the paper or make a single mark.

Then let your eye wander from the foreground object to the middle distance, and from that to the farther-off distances, until you come to the horizon and point of sight, which, as I have said, is the point opposite your eye from where you are sitting.

After you have taken it all in and photographed the scene, as it were, upon your mind, begin to measure and mark off the heights and proportions of the different objects from the distance to that tree trunk in the foreground, using for this purpose your HB pencil very lightly, so that you may be able to erase the marks easily when they are no longer needed.

To be able to measure exactly, you must close one eye, and hold your pencil out at the full extent of your arm firmly in your clenched fingers using the thumb to mark off the length upon the barrel of the pencil as you look past it with one eye at the object you are measuring.

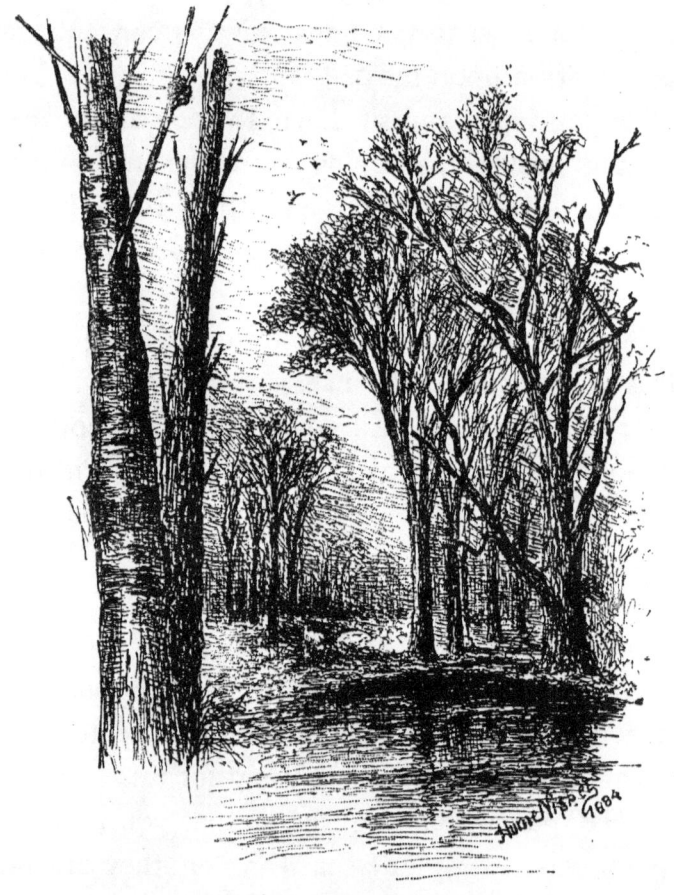

FIG. 6—STUDY OF TREES

Be careful to keep your arm stiffly out, and not bend it as you are moving the pencil about from place to place, or you may make a false measurement; however, a little practice will soon enable you to do this with accuracy.

Your first measurement will be the trunk next to you, noting off different points to it opposite the tops of the objects as they recede in imaginary horizontal lines to the farthest object.

Then measure your spaces between, taking one portion of the trunk as your gauge or test, i.e., see how far up the trunk the width between it and the next tree will reach, and put a dot for it on your paper, and so on, until you have the heights and widths of your picture marked off.

Next come back to your foreground trunk, and measure how many widths it takes from the base to make the height you wish to take in on your paper, then do the same at the top. See how many times its width at that part you require for the width at the base, until you know exactly how much your trunk tapers off. If you measure the birch trunk I have given you here at the top, you will see that it takes about two and a half of the top widths to make the bottom width, and about seven and a half widths at the base to reach the top, also about four times the same width to reach the trunk, which stands to the right of the copy.

When you have satisfied yourself upon these different points and marked them off, look next to the direction, or slant of each tree, and draw lines through the centre. For instance, the birch trunk slopes slightly to the left, and the fir trunk to the right, while the other trunks stand nearly upright ; mark these off correctly.

Then look after the principal boughs, where they branch off and how, and draw a centre line through each ; your landscape is now blocked out, and you must begin your outside outlines.

Leave all the curves and twistings to the last, draw only straight lines along the outside with your HB. Then, when this is done to your satisfaction, take your H pencil, sharply pointed, and begin to put in your details firmly ; delicately erasing the grounding lines, and marking as you go along. The object which I advise you to finish first is the birch tree, next the fir, then the group to the right, and afterwards your distance. But in this matter consult your own inclination entirely, for there are no arbitrary laws about finishing off.

CHAPTER VIII

PROPORTIONS OF THE HUMAN FIGURE

THE first object which a child will attempt to portray, if he gets a pencil or a piece of chalk in his hand, is the human figure ; the aboriginal of

Australia or savage of the South Seas tries invariably to imitate the same object. To ordinary spectators the main interest of a picture or drawing will be the human subject, or the story which it embodies ; and as it is with the child, the savage, and the ordinary spectator, so it must be with the draughtsman—as soon as he possibly can get at a face or a human figure he will attempt the task.

Therefore, at this stage, it may be as well to indulge the student in a desire so universal and natural, and, in order that he may go to work properly, give him the orthodox rules of measurement and proportion.

The ancient and classic proportions of the human figure are seven and a half to eight heads, i.e., from the crown of the head to the under part of the chin is reckoned to be the eighth portion of the man. Also measuring from finger tip to finger tip, when the arms are outstretched to their full extent is exactly the same length as the man from toe to crown—that is, eight heads—so that, allowing two heads for his width of body from shoulder to shoulder, his arms and hands should each be three heads long exactly.

We divide the body into divisions, as, from crown to chin, one head ; from chin to breast, two heads ; from breast to navel, three heads ; from navel to centre, four heads ; from centre to middle of the thigh, five heads ; from middle of the thigh to lower part of kneecap, six heads ; from this to the

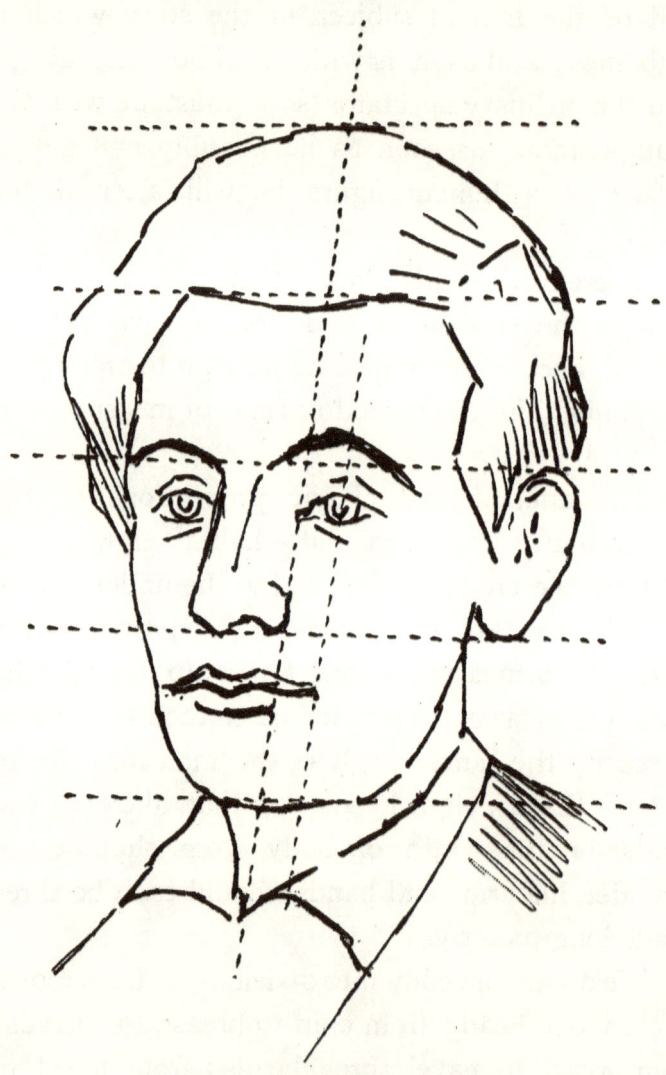

FIG. 7--MEASUREMENT OF A FACE

small of the leg, seven heads ; and from that again to the heel, eight heads.

The arm of a man from shoulder to wrist measures two heads, the hand outstretched is one face-length.

This is the first planning out of the figure. The next task is to divide the head into nose-lengths, which brings us into details.

A man's head is four nose-lengths, thus : From the top of the crown to forehead, one nose ; fore-head, one nose ; nose, and from nose to foot of chin another length ; so the half of a man's head should be at the root of his nose.

A man has thirty-two nose-lengths in his height, and about ten face-lengths. We will take the face-lengths first, so that we may come down by de-grees, as it is only through testing by the different measurements that we can arrive at a certain con-clusion.

From the top of the forehead to the under part of the chin is three noses, or a tenth of the man ; from chin to the pit of the throat, one face ; to under part of breast, one face ; to navel one face ; to near middle, one face ; to upper portion of thigh, one face ; to knee, one face ; to heel, three faces.

The width of a face is two-thirds of its length, i.e., two nose-lengths.

Now to divide the body into nose-lengths : the neck is two nose-lengths ; to below the breast, four and a half ; to waist, three to four ; to hips, four ; to middle of thigh, four ; to knee, one and three-fourths ; to the calf of the leg, two ; to small of the leg, one and two-thirds ; to ankle, one and a third.

The width in diameter of the neck should be two noses, the shoulders eight, waist four, and hips six noses.

The diameter of the legs should be: Top of thigh three nose-lengths ; middle of thigh, two ; at knee one and a half, at the calf two, ankle two, toes one and two-thirds.

The diameter of the arms should be: Top of arms, two nose-lengths ; elbow, one and a half ; below elbow, one and two-thirds ; waist, one ; hand, two.

The ear is one nose-length, and should be horizontally on a line with the nose. The space between the eyes should be half a nose-length ; the nostrils should be the same length in width ; the eyes the same length as the space between them, so that the centre of the eyeball should be perpendicular with the extreme ends of the mouth ; the thickness of the upper lip should be one-eighth of its length, and the lower lip one-fifth.

The length of the foot should be four and a

half-noses, i.e., one half nose-length bigger than the hand.

It is advisable to mark your paper into divisions before you begin to outline your figure at all, beginning with a centre perpendicular line and a centre horizontal line; then make four spaces above and below the horizontal centre. Next draw the outside lines of width—that is, one head space on each side of the centre perpendicular.

You may then look to the position of the arms and legs, and draw lines through where you suppose the centre should be, with their angles; this gives you a ground plan for the pose.

Sketch, after this, lightly, the outlines of the head and body, with what appears to you to be the thickness of the limbs, without attempting either features or curves; make a rough *block* of the whole, allowing yourself plenty of room, as a sculptor would do if beginning to chisel out a block of marble.

When you have done this to your satisfaction begin to measure each part by some other part according to the following rules :

Try how the space between the chin and the throat-pit agrees with the diameter of the neck ; it should be exactly the same.

Compare the diameter of the waist with the

space you have left between the apple of the throat and the crown ; these should also be equal.

From nipple to nipple should be the same as from the wrist to the elbow ; twice the breadth of the hand should be the length of the foot, etc., etc.

If you are drawing from a model, take one portion of that model and measure all the other parts from it, and see how they tally ; do not be content with one portion, but test it again and again by some other portion.   For instance, take a part which is fore-shortened, then fore-thrown out of proportion with the exact measurement, and test what relation it holds with the part which is in repose and can be measured exactly; in this way you can find out how much you have to curtail.

The same rules which govern fore-shortening apply to objects near you and objects more distant. If a man stretches out his foot or hand in advance of his body or other hand and foot, the hand or foot nearest you will appear considerably larger than the hand or foot held back ; photography shows this in a very marked way.

When you are drawing any object, be governed by it alone, and only remember your measurements in a general way. Remember that a fly placed directly in front of your gaze and close to you may appear big enough to cover a distant house, and a man's head, if you get into line with it when he is lying towards you, may be large enough to hide the rest of his body, or at least all of the body beyond the shoulders.

Women and children differ in their measurements from men ; a female head is generally smaller than a male head. The shoulders are narrower in the proportion of six and a half noses to eight of the male, and the hips wider.

Children, again, have much larger heads in proportion to their bodies than men or women. A child of three or four years of age only measures five and a half heads, at nine years of age he measures six heads, at fifteen years six and a half, at seventeen years seven heads.

Again, although as a rule the measurements which I have given *should* be correct, the habits and custom of each individual will make a slight difference. People who exercise their heads more than their muscles will have bigger heads in proportion to the rest of the body ; the arms and legs will also develop or decrease according to exercise. As a rule, athletes and wrestlers have smaller heads than people accustomed to sedentary habits ; people addicted to the table will develop the torso ; beer-drinkers are distinguished mainly by large bodies and weak legs. It is seldom amongst civilised races that we can find perfectly proportioned human beings. The Arabs, although as a rule attenuated, are fairly proportioned ; but the most perfect specimens of humanity that I have seen are the male savages of New Guinea in their natural state ; they are a hardy race, drinking only water when thirsty, industrious, but not overworking themselves ; they work four days out of seven, and enjoy three Sundays each week ; and they eat at regular intervals and never too much at a time, so that in their general habits they more nearly approach to the customs of the early Greeks who must have served as models for those sculptures which guide us in our ideas of the perfection of the human form.

There is no need for me to take up the muscles which cover the human body, as that would only confuse you. If you watch and measure your model carefully you will not go astray in this direction, and while you are drawing it dismiss from your mind everything excepting what lies directly before you on each particular occasion. Never attempt to draw from former experience or prior knowledge, and never attempt to idealise or improve upon your subject ; realism is what must be strictly sought after whether you like it or not. Of course, try to get the best, or most perfect that you can ; for to go and wilfully select, as many of our realists do, a repulsive and uninteresting subject, betrays a mind without any discrimination or sympathy with the feelings of others, unless you have a purpose to teach by doing so.

When you are quite sure that your lines, pose, and proportions are exact, then watch the curves and bulges, and put them in as they appear. You may not know what has caused them at that particular moment, but you will have recorded them all the same.

Some artists, following the example of Michael Angelo and Gustave Doré, study anatomy with the same care that doctors must do. Gustave Doré has shown this in his pictures ; he gives us always the correct play of the muscles ; but as he depended upon his imagination and knowledge, and never used models, his figures lose in consequence much realism and individuality. Still, taking him with all his faults, he must be regarded as the greatest genius of his age, and the worst model for a student to set up as his example ; therefore beware that you never attempt to follow Doré, or Turner in his wild flights of colour, although it is advisable that you should study a little anatomy ; in fact, beware of all geniuses while you are students, and even afterwards try to admire them with great reserve.

CHAPTER IX

ON SHADING

LET us suppose that you have now reached that stage in art when you may begin to aim at expressing yourselves by shadow rather than outline ; not that I would wish you ever to despise outline drawing, because I think there is nothing more expressive and beautiful than fine and delicate outlines, either for landscapes, architecture, or figure drawing ; only, if you are drawing from the round or the life, it is shadow rather than outline which must guide you.

I am supposing that you have learnt, and can appreciate, the full value of a delicate outline ; that you understand a few of the simple and artistic rules of perspective ; that you can make a cup stand up straight, with equal sides ; and that curves, ovals, and circles are no longer an impossiblity for your hand to encounter ; that you can make four sides of a square equal ; that you can find space in your copy to put in *all* the notches of the leaf before you, and also that you do not miss or shun any of the irregularities of the outer or inner lines ; in fact, that you have reached the stage when nothing can come amiss to your pencil to catch, a cup or a cat, a horse or a horse-radish, a monument or a man—all have become legitimate game for your sketch-bag. When you have reached this facile stage you are ready for your charcoal, chalk, and monochrome.

Pencil shading is the most delicate and valuable if it is done properly, that is, used carefully and lightly, and not *rubbed flat* with the finger or a stump. Pencil shading to be a success should either be *hatched*, stippled, or laid on the paper so lightly that the natural grain appears even in the darkest shadow; and to reach this perfection neither bread nor indiarubber should be used ; in fact, if you have made a mistake and have to erase, then you have ruined your drawing.

Turner, Prout, and Harding have left us the best examples of this art, at one time very fashionable, and once more coming into vogue, after nearly half a century of neglect.

Before blacklead was discovered, the old masters used silver points to produce the same effect; that also is again coming into fashion, and for those who like novelties, and do not mind expense, it is a very pretty pastime. To do it properly you must have a prepared ground, so that the silver may mark easily—a thin wash of Chinese white, or whatever pigment you may fancy ; only, as the blacklead requires no preparation, while the same delicacy can be very nearly reached by the careful worker, I would strongly recommend the modern substitute for the ancient silver point to the student who is in earnest.

To 'hatch' is to produce a shadow by broken lines crossed at angles; to 'stipple,' to produce shadow by dots. Both systems require great care and time, but when finished will repay the labour spent.

Perhaps a round ball is the best object to practise shading from; place it where the light falls upon one side, leaving the other in deep shadow, and try to get the gradations and softness of that round object.

To get this, first leave out the highest light, which will be a very small speck, and work into that as lightly as you can until your shadow melts with the light; go over the rest of the ball with this light work until the rest is covered, then gradually darken as you recede from the high light until you make it appear standing out from your surface.

You will discover, as you work, accidental or side lights and reflections; watch carefully their degrees from the other half-shadows, for this is how you learn 'tone' and 'colour.' A white ball or an egg will be the best to practise from first; after that try an apple, pear, or plum, where, besides direct shadow, you will find and must represent colour. If you succeed in these studies you may boldly attempt the human figure, and, laying aside your pencil, use the painter's tool, charcoal.

CHAPTER X

CHARCOAL DRAWING

IN passing from pencil drawing to charcoal, I purposely leave out black chalk drawing as something not worth either describing or practising; it is a filthy medium to work with, and produces neither the delicacy of the pencil nor the colours of the charcoal; therefore, if you do try it in passing, use it exactly in the same way as you have done your blacklead pencil.

But charcoal is different; with a piece of charred vine-branch you can do almost anything, and reach the highest point which black and white can produce. It is easily erased, can be worked about as you like, and as long as you like; it is soft like brush-work, and is the very best prelude to the hog-hair and palette.

Your materials for this work are a few sticks of charcoal, a piece of stale bread, a couple of chamois leathers or paper stumps, and a sheet of charcoal paper.

The bread is used instead of indiarubber, and to pick out lights and half-lights. It is prepared by wetting a small piece and kneading it like dough until it is brought to the proper shape and point as you may require it; it takes the place of a brush, and by using it *feelingly*, will go far to

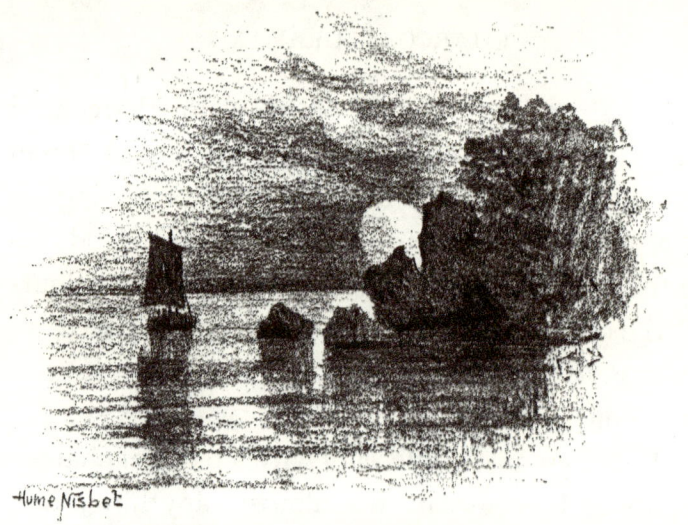

FIG. 8—MOONLIGHT ON SEA-COAST—SPECIMEN OF WHITE
SURFACE AND PENCIL DRAWING

teach you how to use the brush. Wet it only enough to make it knead easily while keeping it stiff.

The charcoal you sharpen or break off to a firm point as you work; a broken or jagged point is the sharpest, and can make the most delicate stroke.

Draw in your spaces and outlines first with
your fine point; then dust off lightly, and begin to

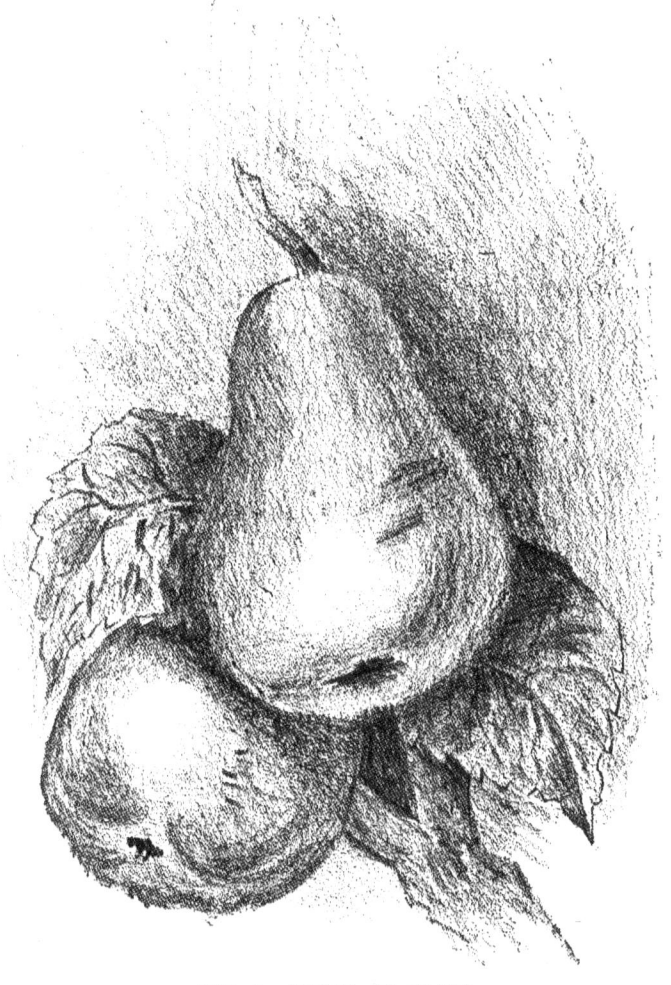

FIG. 9—STUDY OF PEARS

study the shadows, how they fall, what shape they
have, and what space they occupy.

There is no need to exercise the same precision or care with your present material which *fettered* you with your pencil or chalk, for if you make a mistake here, a fillip across the paper with your handkerchief and, presto! your blemish vanishes.

Dash in your heaviest, i.e., your blackest shadows boldly with a square touch, and using your charcoal as flatly and broadly as you can : one decided touch, as nearly the size of the black shadow as you can calculate, and then with your thumb or the stump (I fancy that the thumb is the best and most *feeling* 'softener') trail the charcoal-blotch out to the half-shadows.   I cannot give you a very good specimen in my copy of how to work charcoal, because, before my original sketch has been zincotyped, and reproduced by printer's ink, it must necessarily lose much, if not all, the character both of pencil and charcoal drawing ; still I will draw fig. 8 in pencil and fig. 9 in charcoal, and trust, as I must, to chance that they may be reproduced with sufficient character to show the difference between the two modes of working.

In fig. 10 I have given you a study in tone : 'Twilight,' an old border tower or 'Peel,' with reflections in a pool of water ; this is a blending of pen-and-ink hatching over process work, the nearest

that I can come to 'wash drawings,' with the
process mediums which I am compelled to use for

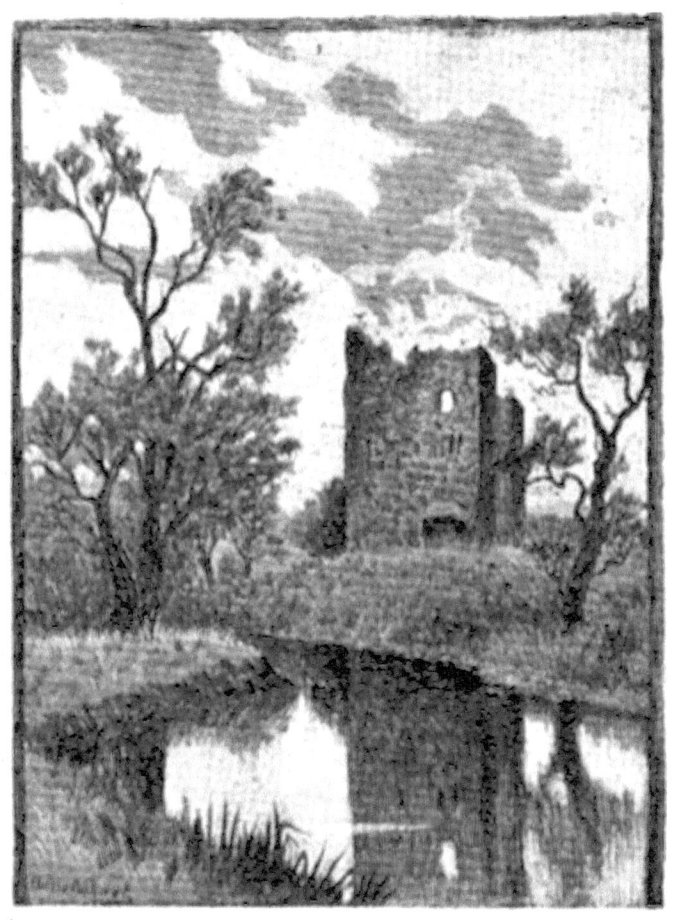

FIG. 10—TWILIGHT—SPECIMEN OF PROCESS-LINED PAPER

the sake of the type, and about which I shall
speak more presently.

To go back, however, to our charcoal study, the main point of which is that there is nothing to control your liberty of action. You can rub it about with your thumb or stump ; lay on heavy masses, soften them, and move them about as you please without let or hindrance, wiping the paper as clean as before you began, which ought to be a source of delight to the worker.

Therefore work confidently and boldly, yet not recklessly, try to make every stroke or rub of some meaning, and a step nearer completion ; get the heavy shadows all in their places, then the half-shadows, and finally soften and blend the whole together, using your stump and bread in a 'patting' manner to lift off the density and leave clearness.

The best mode of regarding a model or object before you, is not to consider what it is like, animate or inanimate, but as something filled with masses of varying degrees and different shapes of light and shadow. If it is a man or a woman, do not regard it as such, or try to make it like what you see it, *en masse* ; look only at the shape and relationship of one portion with the portion lying next to it, until you have succeeded in getting these different portions all in their proper places and degrees ; then stand back and see how they mass together, by comparing your copy with the original.

Now come the finishing and blending of the separate masses, little touches with the charcoal, little wipings with the stump, delicate lifting with the bread. You will have to go over and over again the same spot before you get it up to the exact tone, and as you finish that part, you will find most probably that it has thrown out of harmony some other part ; yet with patience and perseverance you must come to the stage when you can go no further in the improvement of your drawing. It is not finished, for man cannot finish anything thoroughly, but it is done as far as you can do it ; lay down your charcoal and try to be satisfied, as you take up your medium for fixing the drawing so that you may not lose it.

All drawings done in pencil, chalk, or charcoal must be fixed, or made fast to the paper, so that they may not rub off.

Formerly the plan was to spread the drawing upon a tray and pour over it milk, or gum and water, but by this plan much of the work floated from it ; now the colourmen make up a mixture of spirits and gum mastic, which is blown on with a scent spray apparatus in a gentle mist ; this is the best method, and the easiest, and in the long run the cheapest. It is called 'Fixatif,' and can be had at any art colour shop.

CHAPTER XI

PEN-AND-INK ETCHING

THIS is not only a peculiarly pleasant style of work, but also one of the most useful that a student can take up who may wish to gain a livelihood by his art work.

For book and magazine illustrations it is much in vogue, and likely to become more so.

It is difficult to give you a system for this work, as nearly every artist has his own manner of working. The best advice I can give you is to pick out a few good examples, such as you may find in ' The English Illustrated,' 'Harper's,' or 'The Century,' and try to imitate their delicacy and effect. E. A. Abbey is one of the best pen-and-ink workers that you could possibly fix upon to follow. Take a magnifying glass and enlarge his finest lines to about three parts bigger than the reproductions which you will find in 'Harper's,' and try to imitate them that size on a sheet of fine Bristol board, which is about the size he generally works his originals. You will discover, as you examine them carefully, that the lines are mostly short and broken, and that in the cross-hatching they run at angles, never directly across each other, also that they alter the lines to suit each separate object in the picture, and this must be what you have to strive after in your pen work. Follow the direction which the clouds take, alter when you come to the distant mountains, &c., according as they slope ; make your lines lie with the bend of the trees, the appearance of the ground, &c.

Above all, try to *feel* what you are doing, and do not pay so much heed to the mechanism of your work as you must do towards the result, and beware of leaving hard lines or edges, unless it is strictly needful to do so.

The materials required are : the finest-made Bristol boards, a bottle of liquid Indian ink, and two or three different sizes of pens, an etching pen for your very fine lines, whilst any ordinary writing pens such as you generally use will do for the rest.

CHAPTER XII

MONOCHROME

WE have now come to the stage when we must provide ourselves with brushes, and learn how to use them. If you have practised enough with your charcoal, stumps, and bread, you will not find this nearly so difficult as you might imagine.

E

Wash-drawing in Water Colonr

The brushes required for this work are sables,
a large sable or washing-in brush, and several other
sizes ranging from Nos. 10 to 1 ; for very fine
lines a ' rigger.' Use sables instead of camel hair,
for although they are dearer at the start, you will
find them both more satisfactory and cheaper in
the end. I would also advise you to purchase
sables for painting in oil colours, in the tin ferrules,
flat or round ; flat I like best, but that is a matter
entirely of taste, but in the first buying of your
brushes you may as well consider your future work
with the present, and as oil sables work equally
well in water colours, so I recommend them as the
most useful.

A cake of Indian ink and one of sepia must
next be provided, with a pad of 'Whatman's Hand-
wrought Paper,' of medium texture, a glass of
water, and a piece of blotting-paper to absorb the
superfluous moisture out of your brush, with a
plate or piece of porcelain to rub your colours
upon. So we are ready to begin.

After making your drawing lightly but correctly, i.e., the outline only, dip your largest wash
brush into the water and pass it over the surface of
the paper until it is thoroughly wet all over ; when

you have done this, rub down the colour upon your slab or plate until you have enough to give a general wash or half-tone over the paper which you have before moistened. This done, continue to work in the shadows, and half-tones, at the same working wiping out your highest lights with a clean brush and water, drying it *on a handkerchief* where you wish to have the light perfectly clean ; by doing so your shadows and lights will dry soft and rounded, and the general surface becomes as if it had been carefully stippled over.

PART SECOND

PAINTING IN WATER AND OIL COLOUR

CHAPTER I

WATER-COLOUR PAINTING—PERSONAL EXPERIENCE

ALTHOUGH I have had a pretty long and extensive experience in this art of mine, both as worker and teacher, I find it impossible to decide definitely whether it is best for a pupil to begin his colour education with oil or water painting. I began myself in oils, but then my first masters were all oil-painters, and as I was brought up from my very earliest years in the midst of palettes and colour tubes, a hog-hair brush and a piece of chalk or charcoal were much more familiar to me than even a blacklead pencil, while I knew how to blend colours and the laws of harmony long before my mother considered me old enough to begin the alphabet. My mother was a flower-painter and worked in water colours, but as I had professional artists set over me at a very early age, and they all insisted upon my practising in oil, she never interfered.

Therefore, I was fully twenty years of age before I took seriously to water-colour painting ; before that I had mostly dashed off Christmas cards, or put contributions in some friends' albums with the *tender* medium, but when I once really overcame the difficulties and differences between the two mediums, I became passionately en-amoured with pure water-colour painting, a love which still continues.

I tell you these personal experiences at this point because I regard my readers as my pupils, and it is always good for the pupil to know how the teacher learned his trade.

My first efforts in water colours were in body colour, or impasto painting—that is, I worked my water colours as I had been accustomed to use my oils, adding Chinese white to all my other tints, and covering the paper solidly and opaquely ; but I very quickly became dissatisfied with this mode of working, and discarded the white altogether from my paint box ; then the real pleasure began, when I could depend only upon my white paper and transparent washes for my effects. At this time I studied the work of three good masters, viz., Turner, David Cox, and Sam Bough, and through these masters I learned what can be done with a good sheet of paper.

Sam Bough was the man who was nearest to me at the time, for he was alive, in the full zenith of his power, therefore able to give me many valuable hints, which he most generously did. I passed from him to the modern Dutch masters, who, like the Scottish painters, excel in purity of colours.

The Palette required

I think, on the whole, that it will be best for you all to begin where I ended—with pure water colours, and work gradually through the stages of impasto into oil; by doing this you will acquire delicacy of touch, and the keen perception of pure colours, which, once gained, you will never afterwards lose.

In providing yourselves with materials it is best to lay in a complete stock once for all, but in this, of course, circumstances must be considered, therefore I will give you two lists of articles required, the first of which you must have before you can attempt to paint, and the second of which you will be all the better for having if you wish to go along comfortably.

First List.—Strictly needful materials for water-colour painting.

1. Sketch book or block (block is best), size fourteen by ten inches.

2. Sketching stool and seat (octagon).

3. Colour box with four brushes, i.e., wash or sky brush, large and smaller flat sables, and one Siberian hair pencil, or rigger.

4. Colours.—Gamboge, yellow ochre, raw sienna, vermilion, crimson lake, or rose madder, vandyke brown, burnt sienna, cobalt, Antwerp blue, ivory or lamp black, and Chinese white.

That is, eleven colours are strictly required in water-colour painting, but to make up the twelve colours for which the boxes are generally made, I would suggest 'neutral tint,' also that you get half-pan moist colours.

A water-bottle, and dish for holding the water while painting, are also strict necessities.

Second List.—For those who can afford to start in comfort, and who desire a complete outfit.

1. A sketching bag, waterproof, arranged to hold 'block,' colour box, water-bottle, brushes, pencils, &c. Imperial 4to : fifteen by eleven inches.

2. A sketching umbrella, with movable joints.

3. Sketching stool and easel combined.

4. Sketch block (best paper), fourteen by ten inches.

5. Box to hold twenty-five colours.

6. Water-bottle and cup combined.

7. Several assorted sizes of sables.

8. Colours required, with order in which they should be arranged in the box :

1. Lemon yellow ; 2. gamboge ; 3. cadmium yellow ; 4. gallstone ; 5. yellow ochre ; 6. raw sienna ; 7. brown ochre ; 8. raw umber ; 9. burnt umber ; 10. brown pink ; 11. burnt sienna ; 12. Vandyke brown ; 13. brown madder ; 14. purple lake ; 15. sepia ; 16. vermilion ; 17. rose madder ; 18. Indian red ; 19. light red ; 20. terre verte ; 21. sap green ; 22. cobalt ; 23. Antwerp blue ; 24. neutral tint ; 25. lamp black.

These colours may be got in pans or tubes for a beginner : pans are the best, as they keep longer moist, only you must lay in extra, and keep apart, a tube of Chinese white.

A small bottle of oxgall will be found useful to remove grease, or when the colours are apt to run off the paper.

You are now completely furnished for either indoor or outdoor work. Personally, I could not wish a better set of tools, and I dare say that Turner or Cox were not always so well provided when they went out to get their masterpieces. I do not mention one or two colours—such as emerald green, indigo, crimson lake, carmine, &c.—because no artist will ever require these ; they are fugitive, therefore treacherous colours, with the exception of emerald, which tint in its raw state I never saw in Nature, nor do I desire to see it.

CHAPTER II

ON THE BLENDING AND MAKING OF MIXED COLOURS

THE rainbow is the best example which I can set before you to show you how colours are mixed, and what half-tints they produce when blended. The centre is generally yellow, with red on the one side and blue on the other; so red, yellow, and blue are your direct colours.

Towards the red side, as the yellow begins to mix, you find different degrees of orange, growing deeper as the red predominates over the yellow, until you get pure lake.

You know from this that yellow and red produce orange ; lemon yellow and rose madder, bright orange ; raw sienna and madder, orange-brown, &c.; according to the brightness and directness of your primary two colours so will your secondary tints be bright, and *vice versâ*.

As the yellow approaches the blue, green becomes the result. Lemon yellow or gamboge and Antwerp blue or cobalt will make a vivid green, as nearly approaching to emerald as any artist will require. Raw sienna, brown pink, ochre, or umber, with Antwerp blue or cobalt, will produce all the different tones of green which you require and will find in Nature.

As the blue side of the rainbow approaches the sky, it becomes gradually merged into it and lost; but as the red side mixes with the blue of the sky, it becomes purple, therefore you know that blue and red make purple. Lake and cobalt make direct purple, light red or brown madder less vivid, and so on.

Thus you have the primary colours—red, yellow, and blue, and the secondary shades—orange, green, and purple; the other mixed tints—brown, russets, and greys—are formed by different degrees of the three primaries blended together.

Grey in its many varieties is the prevailing tone which pervades all objects and spaces, and in its adroit rendering shows the power and experience of the artist. In the clouds and misty distances, amongst the grasses and foliage, over rocks and boulders, in shadows of faces, and folds of drapery, it is to be found, qualifying and toning down everything.

Harmony and Contrast

Harmony is the proper blending of colours, and contrast is brought about by their complementaries ; for instance a red object will give out green shadows and folds, green will surround itself with red, purple will produce orange-brown shadows, yellow will make a purple background, blue will cause objects directly near to it to become orange; nothing direct, of course, yet tending towards the complementary contrast.

Indeed, it is almost, if not utterly, impossible to set up a direct colour a little distance from you without finding its colour altered and tinged with something else near it ; a blue vase, for instance, will gather about it and into it a host of other tones, and so become a unity, for it cannot be isolated completely ; and it is in this that the painter shows his skill or ignorance when he is copying it. Blue predominates, yet it is only a portion of other colours—orange, brown, green, and grey, grey occupying the largest proportion ; in the case of a blue vase, it will be blue-grey with orange-brown grey surroundings.

A dark-complexioned man or woman can wear with advantage yellow or orange, by reason of the yellow and orange which predominate in their complexions. A fair complexion is best seen to advantage with delicate tones of blue or green, by reason of the purples and greys which predominate in the flesh tints.

CHAPTER III

GOOD STUDIES FOR WATER COLOURS

ONE of the very best studies anyone can possibly have to get the value and purity of grey is an oyster-shell or a fresh herring.

Set either of them up a little way distant and where the light will strike upon them, and try to imitate the prismatic blendings which you see before you. To do this, you will require your most delicate yellow, lemon, with rose madder and cobalt, also a little raw sienna and terre verte; and if you work conscientiously over this task—whether you produce the oyster-shell and fish or not does not matter much—you will discover how to form silvery grey, and be able to paint a sun-lighted mist, such as that great picture of Turner's 'Sun Rising in a Mist,' a picture which I have copied more than once, and which hangs in the National Gallery, London.

For direct colour-blendings, set up a bunch of assorted flowers, white predominating, with bright yellows, reds, and blues amongst the green leaves and white blossoms ; mix them so that the yellow flowers sometimes touch the red and sometimes the blue, as well as the white, and as you paint you will soon find out the contrasts for yourselves— that portion of the yellow flowers which lies against the blue will appear pallid and green, while the blue will appear purplish ; that portion which rests against the red will show up orange, while the red will become more violet ; the green leaves, also, will become browner or greyer as they approach the direct colours.

Green is the most accommodating of all colours, therefore it is the most liberally scattered through- out Nature. It blends with and intensifies the blue of the sky, the grey of the distance, the silver glint of the stream, the gold of the cornfield, or the glow of the flower garden ; in fact, green is the very best background which we could possibly have for all other colours, direct or blended, not because it is green, but because it is like the chameleon, and changes its tone continually, according to what it is placed against, so that we seldom find vivid green for long anywhere ; it is the grand mediator and adjuster of all discordancy.

One of the simplest and most picturesque of subjects is an old cottage ; the specimen which I give here for you to copy has been sketched in

summer-time, about the month of July, with the
sun shining at the back of the group, and casting
their shadows half-way over the roadway. (See
fig. 11.)

The sky is grey and cloudy with warm lights.
I find that I used cobalt, rose madder, and yellow

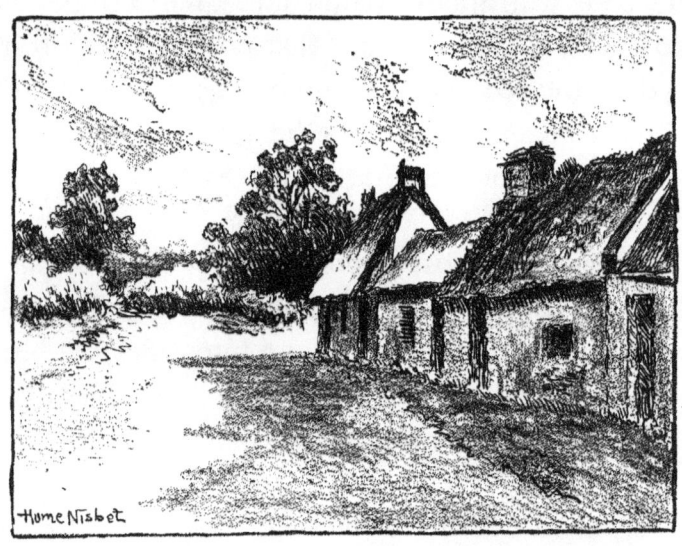

FIG. 11—STUDY OF COTTAGES

ochre in this sky—cobalt and madder, with very
little ochre in the cloud-shadow, with more ochre
in the lights, the white of the paper making the
lights. The green of the trees, which are dark, I
produced with brown pink, and Antwerp blue in
the middle distance, raw umber and cobalt in the
more distant ones. The sunlit portion of the road

has yellow ochre and light red in it, while to the shadows I added cobalt, raw umber, and rose madder. The walls of the cottage are warm-toned sepia, raw sienna, light red, and cobalt ; the roof, different degrees of brown and green, in which I used Vandyke brown, burnt sienna, brown madder, with sap green and gamboge.

Paint this sketch in the following manner :—

A general light wash over the whole picture with yellow ochre, very faintly laid on with plenty of water ; while it is drying blend in rose madder and ochre softly where the lights are to be, then cobalt, yellow ochre, and rose madder with the shadow portions of the clouds ; by this means you will get your sky effect soft, and without hard edges—a very important point in water colours.

Sky-work.—Aim always at having it as transparent and clear as you possibly can. The other parts of the picture paint in after your first one is dry, although, if you like, you may put in the light portions of the roadway while the other parts are drying, making it darker than the light portions of the sky. After this, put in the local colouring by broad washes with your largest sables, leaving the details until the last—that is, always look to getting your masses with their gradations and degrees of shadow done before you put in details. Use no white in this sketch; if you cover over some of your light places accidentally, take your brush, charged with clean water, and wipe it out again.

In fig. 12 you will find a glowing sunset, with an old wreck lying ashore. The sun is orange, i.e· rose madder and gamboge, different degrees of orange and yellow, with touches of vermilion and

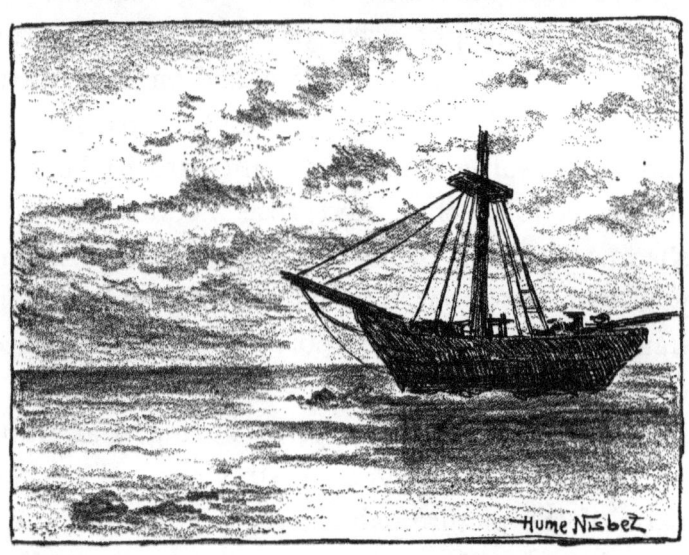

FIG. 12—A WRECK

yellow ochre; in the shadow portion rose madder, yellow ochre, and cobalt. The sea is purple, except where the sun glow passes down, which is vermilion, lake, and orange; the wreck and sands are in deep shadow of brown madder, Vandyke brown, and cobalt. This is also a transparent water colour, and will require a great number of washes and wiping out to bring it up strong and clear.

Indeed, you must make up your minds to work over a transparent water colour a great many times, and with delicate washes, if you wish to make it pure ; and one comfort you may take while you work, that, as long as you do not introduce Chinese white, or lay on your washes too opaquely, you can always rectify an error by wiping out. To do this a clean brush and water is generally sufficient ; but if you wish to take out a sharp light, pass your brush first over the place, and then use your handkerchief and rub it out quickly ; this direct wiping out, however, is best left to the last, when you come to put in your shadow details with sharp touches, and see where the lights are to come out.

The final advice I have to give you is to flood your pictures often with faint washes, where the water predominates, and wait until the paper dries before putting on your next wash, that is, after the first general working over. As you get on you will discover new secrets and methods for yourselves, the result of accidents mostly, that will be of infinite service to you, but which no master can teach you unless he works before you.

F

CHAPTER IV

IMPASTO PAINTING IN WATER COLOUR

FIG. 13 is an impasto painting ; that is, done directly with the mixture of Chinese white. I give it as the half-way to oil painting, which we will take up

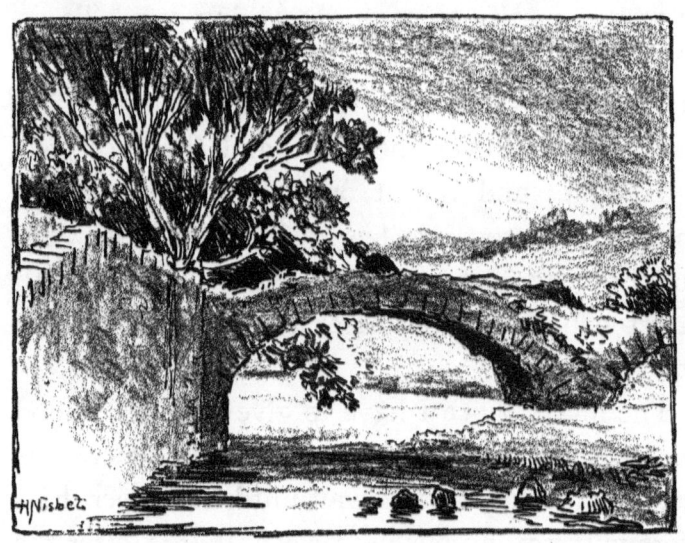

FIG. 13—AN OLD BRIDGE

next. It is the system by which scene painting and fresco work is done.

The light portion of the sky is painted with Chinese white, warmed by a little ochre and laid on thickly ; the shadow parts of the clouds are produced by Chinese white, raw umber, cobalt, and light red.

In the hill and trees are different blending of green and ochres, with white added ; on the old bridge, blendings of purple, russet, and grey, also with white. The water is treated in the same way as the sky.

Do this study quickly and decidedly, and, if possible, at one working, except where you have to add shadows and details ; these you do after the picture is thoroughly dry, and make every stroke or wash tell at once, as it will be spoilt if much worked over. If you manage this successfully you will be ready for oil paints.

CHAPTER V

OIL PAINTING

WE have now come to the stage when, if you pay great attention to the hints I am about to give you, we may bid each other good-bye as far as the use of paints and brushes is concerned.

Of course, I have not touched upon many sub-jects which come within the compass of Art, i.e., modelling in wax and clay, wood-carving and engraving, decorating, leather work, and the many other modes by which the devotees of art express themselves. These branches I may take up at some future time, meantime let us confine ourselves to the subject in hand—painting.

There are a few things which must be carefully avoided in oil painting, and which are not to be met in water-colour painting, and these I shall mention first.

For instance : You will not find any more seductive colours than the rich, transparent browns which are made from asphaltum, nor any that will ruin your pictures more quickly. Avoid asphaltum, bitumen, and mummy, for they will all crack your picture in a thousand places, and use instead Caledonian brown, Cappah brown, Cassel earth, Cologne earth, Vandyke brown, or Mars brown. These are safe colours, because they are mostly composed from earths, and all earths, such as ochre, Venetian reds and umbers are always enduring, and what the old masters used in their pictures ; yet I will admit that while working you will get no colours so perfect or so easy to manage as are the asphaltum preparations.

There are other colours which are also to be avoided, because they are so short-lived and fleeting, that is, they will fade and vanish when exposed to the light in a very short space of time ; these fading colours are mostly made from vegetables, i.e., dyes extracted from leaves, flowers, roots, gums, &c.

Of these I would mark out specially crimson lake, gamboge (this gum in water colour is fairly sound, but not in oil), Indian lake, Italian pink, and yellow lake.

The chromes, as a rule, are generally best to be left out of your colour list, as they will all *blacken* in time through exposure to the light and air.

I will give you now a good and comprehensive list to choose from, which are all more or less lasting, and which may be used with comparative safety with each other. I add to each their qualities and effects upon a canvas in the course of time.

1. *Flake white.*—This is the best preparation of white we can have for general purposes ; it is made from lead, and, like all lead preparations, will grow darker in time, but this cannot be avoided. From experience I am convinced that we have no better artistic white than flake white.

2. *Lemon yellow.*—This colour is very enduring, and well worth the money.

3. *Aureolin.*—This colour is almost perfect, and will do almost as well for glazing purposes as most yellow lakes.

4. *Strontian yellow.*—Like lemon yellow, this is an extremely safe and enduring colour.

5. *Yellow ochre.*—An earth, therefore perfect, and the most useful colour an artist can have.

6. *Brown ochre, Roman ochre, and transparent gold ochre.*—All under the same class as yellow ochre.

7. *Raw sienna.*—This is a colour you must never run short of.

8. *Cadmium, yellow, pale, and orange.*—All extremely useful colours for sunsets and bright scenes.

9. *Vermilion.*—That this is a safe colour may be proved by the paintings, still extant and vivid, upon the masks and outer coverings of the Egyptian mummies.

10. *Light red, Venetian red, or terra rosa.*—These are all burnt ochres.

11. *Indian red.*—A very powerful earth.

12. *Rose madder, pink madder, madder lake, &c.*—These are all so nearly alike in their colours and quality that you may make your choice.

13. *Burnt sienna.*—Like raw sienna, this is a colour you cannot dispense with.

14. *Brown madder, Rembrandt's madder, &c.*—You are perfectly safe with the madders.

15. *Terre verte.*- I use this ochre, or earth, mostly everywhere throughout my pictures, and feel lost when I have to do without it.

16. *Raw umber.*

17. *Burnt umber.*

18. *Vandyke brown, Cologne earth, Caledonian*

brown, &c.—Either of these browns will serve, only they are all slow dryers, and sometimes may require a little sugar of lead added to them to make them dry.

19. *Cobalt, ultramarine, or new blue.*—Cobalt is the best for those who cannot afford genuine ultramarine.

20. *Antwerp blue.*—This colour stands the effect of time and weather better than Prussian blue.

21. *Lamp-black.*

Medium, or magilp, may be used moderately throughout the picture, with the addition of a little turpentine.

Sugar of lead may be added to the slow-drying colours, only as little as possible, as it acts injuriously upon them afterwards ; however, with rose madder in its pure state and Vandyke brown, it is impossible to do altogether without it, siccatif, or some kind of drying oil. Japan gold size is the quickest drying medium, but whether it is any the better for this quality is a doubtful question. One advice I would strongly impress upon you at the beginning, and that is : use as little oils, dryers, medium, or turpentine as you possibly can throughout the different stages of your picture, just sufficient to moisten your tube colours and make them spread over the canvas or board, and lay them on as dryly and thickly as you can do with comfort to yourselves. Make yourselves comfortable always, and at perfect ease with your work, brushes, canvas, and subject, and you are in the surest path towards success.

The palette is the next point to study ; a mahogany oval one will be the best, say about twelve inches, which is a very useful size. Clean your palette each night when you finish work, and polish it carefully with a little medium or magilp and a rag before you lay it away, and you will find it a pleasure to take up again.

'The Sketching Box' is a very useful size both for indoor and outdoor work, thirteen inches by eight and a half inches. It is best to purchase an empty box and fill it with the colours which you think you will require, although the other fittings-up are generally pretty satisfactorily arranged, i.e., bottle of turpentine (instead of linseed oil I would suggest a large tube of medium), tin dipper, knife, a couple of flat sables, small sizes, ten or twelve assorted sizes of *flat* hoghair brushes, one pencil or rigger, and a portcrayon, with a stick or two of charcoal.

With regard to your brushes, there can only be one way of taking care of them, and that is to wash them out most carefully each time they are used with soap, hot water, and a pinch of Hudson's Extract in the first water ; afterwards rinse them thoroughly out with clean cold water and dry them with a towel, pressing them into shape before laying them away. If you wash them in turpentine they will become hard and rot away in a short time. If you attempt to use any kind of non-drying oil, such as paraffin, sweet or olive oil, you will get into such a helpless and hopeless mess, that oil painting will become instead of a pleasure an abhorrence to you; therefore, as you value your peace of mind, never attempt to try any of these lazy expedients.

Canvas is the best to work upon, therefore provide yourselves at the beginning with a few canvases on wedged frames; for landscapes fourteen by ten inches is a very good size, and for figure subjects twelve by ten inches will do very nicely.

Your combined sketching easel and stool will be all that you require for ordinary work, but if you intend to stand indoors, a very good easel is the ' Universal Deal Easel,' six feet high

Set your easel up with your canvas upon it, and sketch in your subject with charcoal. I give you a fairly good subject to begin upon, an old castle in the moonlight (Fig. 14); it is a grey subject, with brown shadows, greenish, i.e., terre verte and raw sienna half tones and silvery high lights. When painting a moonlight such as this, you put in the same variety of colouring as in a daylight scene, only in a lower tone, and in a much more modified degree. Grey enters more directly into your picture than it would do by day ; the consequence of this grey overpowering the local colouring in the high and half lights will be to make the shadows browner and warmer in their tones.

Divide your work as nearly as possible into three stages.

The first stage will consist of drawing the subject and covering the shadows, and getting rid of the glare of the new canvas. For this particular study I would advise you to use only burnt sienna and burnt umber with a little medium and turpentine, and a flat hoghair brush, not too large ; do not go into too many details, but limit yourselves in this working to the degrees and masses of broad shadows. We call this dirtying the canvas, and the mode of work *scumbling*, that is, to use the colour as transparent as possible, leaving the canvas to shine through.

Second stage.—This is the working stage, during which you must build up your picture to the last detail with solid colour, using as little medium in the process as you possibly can.

Set your palette in the following order, and with the following colours for this moonlight : Flake white, strontian yellow, yellow ochre, light red,

rose madder, raw umber, Vandyke brown, brown
·madder, terre verte, and cobalt.

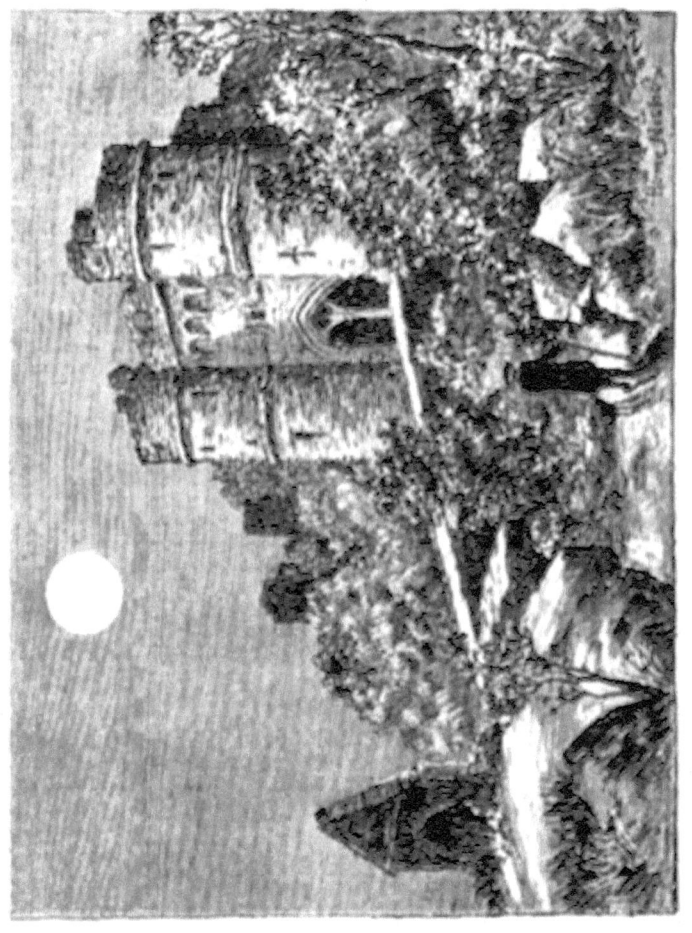

FIG. 14—RUINS OF A CASTLE

The moon is high, therefore pale, and that
is the first object which you must put in, as it is
your brightest piece of colour. Mix flake white

and strontian yellow for that, and put it in solidly and thickly.

The sky which surrounds the moon is greenish grey. To make this colour use cobalt, terre verte, raw umber, and a little rose madder ; blend these about on your canvas, taking touches of pure colour as you require them from your palette, and mix them together as you go along on the canvas ; thus you will get variety of tint as you get your gradations of tone, from the moon to the horizon, which will gradually grow darker as it recedes from the light— darker and colder in colour, i.e., bluer and greyer. Round the pale lemon-white moon, the grey ought to be a little more purple, verging to green grey, and from that to blue grey.

Next begin to paint your middle distance, the trees, and castle. For this portion add to the colours that are already ranged out on your palette, raw sienna.

For the foliage, terre verte and raw umber with a little cobalt will be required, along with flake white for the light parts.

In the castle you will use flake white, umber, raw sienna, light red, and terre verte ; for the moon-lit portions, the half-shadows will have more terre verte and raw umber, while in the deep shadows you will use brown madder and raw sienna with a little terre verte.

When you come to the foreground, add to your palette burnt sienna and Antwerp blue, and at this point discard your cobalt, which is only used for distant greens. The terre verte also you can do without at this part, blending raw sienna with Antwerp blue for your more vivid greens, burnt sienna or raw umber with Antwerp blue for your less vivid greens ; brown madder, Vandyke brown, and burnt sienna for your deepest shadows ; and a mixture of white with the different local colours for your lights.

Third stage.—The picture is now complete as far as colouring and detail are concerned, but it looks *dry* and hard. This is the stage where you soften edges, make distances misty and vague, and shadow portions rich and juicy, bringing your picture into a unity, so that no harsh discordancy may catch and offend the eye.

For the distant effect you use a *scumble* of grey, with medium enough to render it semi-transparent ; go over the harsh portions, blurring them a little so that they may recede gradually into the distance from the foreground.

After this is done to your satisfaction, you will *glaze* the foreground. To *glaze* means to use transparent colours with medium, such as raw and burnt siennas, rose and brown madder, Vandyke brown, and Antwerp blue. These are the purely transparent colours, which serve to give depth and richness of effect to the shadow portions of your foreground.

Finally, you may see the necessity of putting in some sharp lights and shadow-lines ; for these use your sables and rigger. I have presumed that up to these last touches you have been using only your hoghair brushes, and of these the largest you can find comfortable ; put in as much of your details in the middle stage with these hoghair brushes as you can, and what you cannot do easily leave till the finishing all sharp touches ; by this I mean do not introduce your sable-brushes or rigger until the very last, if you wish to produce good, firm, and solid work.

Last piece of advice in this picture—keep plenty of soft, well-worn cotton or linen rags beside you to wipe your palette and brushes with, and wipe them always as clean as possible before dipping them into the turpentine, which you keep in your dipper. Wipe the brushes carefully afterwards, also before using fresh colour, and when you require to *thin* your colours use as little turpentine and medium as you can, and always mix them together in equal portions ; otherwise, if the turpentine predominates your surface will dry flat and dim ; if the medium predominates it will be too glossy, and also run the risk of cracking.

In flower painting and fruit painting begin and go on with the picture in the same way—first, second, and third stages, only be very sure of your drawing always.

Many ladies like to paint on porcelain and plaques. If on porcelain, you must use your colours the same as if you were painting in pure water colours, transparently and by thin washes, without considering the stages of legitimate painting in oil, for you want the porcelain background to serve the purpose of white, therefore you must use your colours very thin, and with as little white as possible, and no hoghair brushes; work here always softly and faintly.

If, however, you are painting solidly upon jars, terra-cotta plaques, or American cloth, paint exactly as I have told you in the present moon-light study, leaving the ground, however, as your background, and choosing your colours and objects to match the background.

Animal painting is done exactly in the same way, according as you wish to make an ornament of your subject or a picture.

CHAPTER VI

FIGURE PAINTING IN OIL

THE palette required for flesh tints is :—Flake white, strontian yellow, aureolin, yellow ochre, raw sienna, vermilion, light red, rose madder Indian red, raw umber, Vandyke brown, burnt sienna, brown madder, terre verte, and cobalt blue.

In a fair complexion the purples predominate in the shadows, rose madder, terre verte, and cobalt; while in the lights, aureolin, and ochre with vermilion, and rose madder are chiefly used.

In a dark complexion, green and more intense purple blend about, terre verte, raw sienna, brown madder, and cobalt; while the lights are combinations of direct yellows, ochre principally, and sometimes direct touches of strontian yellow; the deepest shadows are made rich and warm with burnt sienna, brown madder, and Vandyke brown.

Divide your working into three stages as in landscapes, the first to be the drawing and rubbing in with monochrome. If the subject is very fair, use in this working light red. If dark, use burnt sienna and Vandyke brown.

In the second stage, begin with your deepest shadows, next your highest lights, and work the half-tones into each. Lay on your colours always firmly and solidly, and in the second stage keep your lights well under, i.e., a shade or so less vivid than you intend to finish them.

The draperies and accessories are easily managed, if you have them before you and watch them narrowly; if there are tartan checks, or patterns upon them, leave the markings always until the last, and until you are quite sure that you have got the ground colour with the folds correctly represented.

PART THIRD

HINTS ON GENERAL ART

CHAPTER I

DIFFERENT MODES OF PAINTING—PASTEL WORK

As crayon or pastel work has come much into use and fashion of late years, and as it is besides a very easy and fascinating mode of expressing the ideas of the student, I give here a few hints as to the working of it.

Any roughened paper, canvas, or vellum will do for the ground, so that it has grip or 'tooth' enough to 'catch' and hold the colours; and as it has lately developed, artists prefer the very coarsest material they can get, so that they may be able to lay on their pastels in thick masses. Formerly, crayon drawing was smoothed about and blended one colour with the other, until the whole looked velvety and soft, but now they have shown in recent exhibitions that strength and ruggedness may be obtained as much with the dry medium as with oil and water colour, which has lifted the art of pastel drawing out of the ' pretty ' grade into the firm and artistic.

The first thing to get is a complete set of good French pastels. In this I would strongly advise the largest assortment sold, for, unlike oils and water colours, you do not require to make your half tones so much as to know how to harmonise them, and this you can only accomplish by some practice.

You may require a stump, as in chalk drawing, at first, but as you proceed you must come to depend altogether for softening and blending of the colours upon your fingers ; for the colours in their dry state are so easily ' blurred,' that the stump is not nearly sensitive enough.

Spread your box of pastels before you, with your canvas or prepared paper stretched on a board on your easel, and then, after you have drawn your subject out with charcoal or chalk, begin at once, boldly and rapidly, as you might do with your oils, only in this case you may not proceed by stages ; the effect must be wrought up as quickly as possible.

Your first mistake and constant tendency will be towards pitching too high and vivid a scale ;

therefore I would advise you to begin at the deepest shadows and work towards your light, keeping your colours always below nature a shade or two, for it is so easy to add light.

Do not attempt to work too smoothly; lay on your colours in strong and rugged masses, shifting and blending as little as possible. Work broadly, massively, and sombrely, leaving the harmonising and light sharp touches until your picture is covered, then you may play with the subject and finish it with work as long as you like.

The best possible intention to have in your mind while pastel drawing, is to suppose that you are doing mosaic-work with small pieces of coloured stones to make a harmonious whole, and as you would do if you were placing the tiny pieces together, so press down your colour definitely and in its pure state, leaving the blending together to the last stage.

I do not think that this revived art of pastel drawing will endure very long, and I found this belief upon consideration of the difficulties which surround it: (1.) The extreme difficulty of being able to 'fix' the colours without blemishing them, or at least losing some of their most delicate qualities. (2.) That it cannot be worked in the open air, because the wind will blow off the lighter surface-dust finish; therefore it must be worked in the studio or under cover. (3.) Because the artist cannot do more than imitate the qualities of either oil or body water colours, unless he aims entirely at making the soft and unnatural texture of the old style of crayon drawings, which at the best is somewhat insignificant art.

There are methods of fixing it, such as 'steaming,' 'spray,' or floating the paper upon the back in various preparations, but in each of these there is danger of destroying the most valuable qualities of the work. The best way, therefore, is to frame and cover the drawing with glass as soon as it is done.

Yet, fine and rapid effects can be wrought with crayons with less trouble than either with water or oil colours; therefore, if used for the purpose of making preparatory studies which are not intended to be preserved, it is a most useful and also a delightful medium for the artist in his studio, to make hasty studies from models as suggestions for after work, or the working out of a first idea. In this way I would compare pastel in painting to modelling clay in sculpture, and recommend its use strongly in this sense, and no other.

CHAPTER II

SCENE PAINTING, OR DISTEMPER

I WOULD advise all students, who wish to distinguish themselves as landscape painters particularly, to try to get some practice at the painting of stage scenery, as it is one of the finest exercises for giving the artist a free hand, a bold decided touch, and a quick eye for effects. Personally I have done a good deal of it in various forms, such as stage scenery, photographers' backgrounds, wall decorations, &c., and do not know what I should have done without this practice, both in my pictures and my illustrations.

If you cannot get any preliminary work to do under the eye of a qualified scenic artist, get a large stretcher, say ten or twenty feet long and eight or fifteen feet high, and stretch upon it a piece of sheeting or unbleached cotton. Wet this over before tacking it upon your stretcher, and after it dries make a solution of glue-size and whiting of about the consistency of cream; coat your sheet carefully over with this. It will require two coats of this mixture, perhaps three, before it is ready for your picture.

When dry and taut, sketch out the design with charcoal, and then mix up your colours.

Use powder colours, mixing them with water in separate pots with just sufficient gum or glue-size to fix them, and set them handy upon your table or bench. Your white, with which you mix and blend all your colours, may either be powdered Chinese white solved with water and a little gum added, or common whiting fixed with glue-size. Chinese white is the easiest to work with, as it does not change so much as whiting in the drying, but it is much more expensive.

If you use whiting, you must paint your scene much darker and stronger than you intend it to appear when dry, say five tones lower with whiting and two tones lower with Chinese white.

Your medium for working, i.e., the liquid, will be weak gum-water, or weak size ; for if you make it too strong, your colours will dry all sorts of tones, and, what is worse, will look glazed and hard, besides cracking off in flakes at the least rolling or bending of the canvas.

Use large hoghair brushes, for sky work pound brushes, sash tools and fitches for the finer work.

Before you begin, make up your mind exactly what you intend to do, for you must not stop to plan out until your entire ground is covered ; then dash away, and get over all the broad work while it remains wet—sky, distance, middle distance, and foreground—get all in that you possibly can, excepting, perhaps, the finishing touches of the foreground, before you stop the first working.

After this let it dry thoroughly, and then you will be able to see how much it requires to finish it, leaves, bark of trees, branches, distant houses or ornaments, &c., over the interiors.

It is hard work—as hard, perhaps, as white-washing ceilings or walls; but it is decidedly in-vigorating, pleasant, and useful, as you will discover when you begin your next picture.

CHAPTER III

FRESCO PAINTING AS PRACTISED BY THE ANCIENTS

To achieve success in true fresco painting, or *Buon Fresco*, the artist must have a certain knowledge of the chemistry of colours, for the difference between fresco and distemper painting lies in the fact that you are using lime instead of Chinese white or whiting along with your colours, therefore you can only use such colours as may not be in any way affected by the lime, which considerably limits your stock; also you must have experience enough to paint your pictures entirely, or as much of the

ground as you decide to colour, from the beginning
to the last stroke of your design, in *one day*, while
the mortar is fresh and wet ; there can be no after-
touches in a true fresco. It is in this decided way
that such masters as Raphael, Michael Angelo,
Leonardo da Vinci, &c., proved their great knowledge, vast assurance, and power.

The method of this work is as follows: As
much of the wall as the painter can work upon in
one day is plastered over before he begins, and
then on the wet mortar he paints his design, using
as his medium a lime solution instead of size or
gum ; as the mortar dries, it absorbs the colours,
and by its properties of carbonate of lime and
silica becomes crystallised and firm ; yet, as the
climate of England is unfavourable to the preser-
vation of this mode of work, unless as an experiment, it is useless to the English artist.

Fresco secco is a substitute for the real system,
and is worked by coating the dry plaster with lime
water and then working upon it ; but as this has
nothing to recommend it beyond ordinary distemper, it is needless to describe it further in this
manual.

CHAPTER IV

MINIATURE PAINTING, &C.

MINIATURE painting is almost a lost art since photography has so ably taken its place. It is a labour requiring great patience and delicacy, as well as talent, to bring it to perfection ; so that coloured photographs generally are preferred, not only for their greater accuracy, but for their cheapness.

The ground of a miniature is ivory, roughened slightly by powdered pumice, and the water colours are laid on not by washes, but by careful *hatching* and *stippling*, i.e., by obliquely crossed lines, and small dots of different colours worked side by side with the ground showing through, or over one another when shadow is required.

ENCAUSTIC, OR WAX PAINTING

There are various methods of working in this art. 1st. The design is engraved on a surface of ivory with a metal point or *estrum*, afterwards coloured and varnished with melted wax. 2nd. By means of a heated metal instrument like that used for soldering lead and coloured wax sticks, so that they are blended into each other. 3rd. By making

the wax soluble with an oil, and painting it with
brushes as any other oil painting, the whole when
finished being hardened by exposure to heat, and
afterwards polished by rubbing.

ENAMEL PAINTING

This is an expensive and most uncertain mode
of expressing ideas, yet for its enduring qualities
it is valuable. It is usually painted upon copper
or gold, and has to be fixed and brought out by
'firing.' The ground is prepared by covering the
surface with powdered white enamel, after which
it is melted in a furnace, and when cooled, painted
with powdered colours of metallic oxides mixed
with flux and a prepared oil, and applied with
brushes ; this done it is once more fired, and if the
painter has experience enough to reckon accurately
upon the results, it comes out all right ; if not, he
must not lose patience : it is all chance work.

China painting is similar to enamel painting, in
so far that the colours are limited, and have to be
calculated by what they will come out of the furnace, rather than by what they appear when laid on
to the china. The prepared colours can be obtained from any colourman, with full directions
attached.

CHAPTER V

ON THE COPYING OF PICTURES

IT is indispensable to a young artist to exercise himself some time in copying those masterpieces which adorn picture galleries in this country and abroad.

I think no young painter should consider his art education complete unless he has spent two or three years at discriminate copying of good and useful pictures.

By discriminate copying, I mean that he ought to select, or get selected for him, not only the pictures which are likely to be most useful to him in his own particular bent, but the best portions of each picture, leaving the other pictures and other parts alone.

In oil colours and in landscapes, for instance, I would not advise anyone to do more than make a very rough study of Salvator Rosa, yet I would say, make one hasty study, and try to accomplish what he did in the given time ; i.e., in one sitting. Salvator Rosa will teach you vigour, if nothing else. I am Philistine enough to think that you will not learn much from Constable's work, yet his 'Cornfield' has some qualities about it which may help you on. Do not trouble about any of the old masters past Gainsborough as regards landscape, except, perhaps, Teniers, and some of the Dutch painters, such as Vandervelde and Hobbema ; also perhaps, if you wish it, one of Claude.

Painters before the days of Claude Loraine did not paint from nature, or even care to imitate nature ; they devoted themselves mostly to the figure subjects, and composed backgrounds of impossible trees, and lakes which were not water, however pretty they may have looked.

Claude did not paint much nature either, although he went the length of making studies from nature. Turner, also, did not paint his oils from nature direct, therefore, they are not of so much benefit to students as are his water colours, and of these his *unfinished* studies.

In oils, there are only two pictures of Turner's which I can conscientiously recommend to the art student as useful, and these are his ' Sun rising in a Mist ' and ' Crossing the Brook.' Personally, I have copied a number of others, but I need not have taken the trouble after I had finished those two as yet unspoilt specimens.

Gainsborough I can recommend both in his landscapes and his figures. He is free, rich, and careful in all his work ; perhaps the greatest of English artists in all its branches. George Morland, also, after Teniers, is a good man to make studies from ; they will both teach you precision of touch, quickness, and ease, with a fine silver colour, and prevent you, perhaps, from falling into the modern French 'slough' of formless ease and paint, into which so many of our young painters plunge headlong before they are a quarter prepared for going through it.

In water-colour landscapes, the three men most worth studying in the National Gallery at present are Girtin, Turner, and David Cox. Copy as many of their *unfinished studies* alternately as you have leisure to do ; studies of sea and sky first, wings of birds, trunks and branches of trees, and as much of that sort of thing as you can cram into your mind ; and your education as a landscapist will be pretty well complete.

Copying the works of great masters is like playing the scales to a musician, and ought to be done in the same way, that is, a tree, or piece of rock or group out of a landscape, rather than the landscape itself ; a hand, or a foot, or a head, or piece of drapery, rather than the composition as a whole. Take the most excellent portions of each particular master, for you may depend upon it that no single master is perfection all through, but must have some weak portions throughout a large composition ; therefore, as the student does not want to learn the weakness, but only the strength, of the master, it is needful for him to make selections, otherwise a great deal of his time will be wasted on useless copying.

For animal painting make a careful study of the earlier work of Sydney Cooper and Sir Edwin Landseer; the style of the latter perhaps inclines just a little towards prettiness, yet his ease and juiciness of colour are wonderful, and his *surface manipulation* almost as complete as that of Teniers.

George Morland's pigs and dray-horses cannot well be surpassed; also his old cottages and stables possess many fine qualities of conventional colour and dexterity.

For figure painting it becomes a harder matter to advise you upon what pictures to choose, as there are so many masters, ancient and modern, who possess special qualities to recommend them; best take a regular course of part studies, a head or single figure, or at the most a male, female, and infant from each; begin with Leonardo da Vinci and follow down to Gainsborough. Do not trouble, unless you like, about Raphael, i.e., what you find in our National Gallery; he is a matchless master, I will admit, but too smooth in his finish for a young student to learn much from.

Try a head from Leonardo, and a figure or two from Murillo or Velasquez, a head or bit from

Salvator Rosa.   Pass over Tintoretto; he is like our own Turner, splendid, but filled with faults, therefore of no use to a student; pause and turn back to some of the pre-Raphaelites, then take a turn at that master of all masters, Rembrandt.   I am mentioning the painters in the rotation I wish you to take them, the cold with the hot, the stiff with the lavish, and so on.

Take that 'Ecce Homo' by Guido, and after that, part of the 'Dead Christ,' with the Virgin Mother by Francesco Francia; then take one or two of Rubens' fat women, with their flaky necks and robust proportions; go next to Gainsborough's portraits, and then finish up with a nude study from Etty.

In the foregoing course, I have planned out a good three years' work for even the most energetic student during the days and hours allowed for painting.   If he is able to get through this course before that time, he can look round and take what else he fancies, because I reckon that he will then be in a position to know his own art necessities.

I should not advise any student to copy longer than three years at most, and during this time I expect he shall also be either working direct from nature in the fields during the rest of the time, if a landscapist; or working from models if he means to become a figure painter, and practising hard also during his evenings at anatomy, for without a perfect knowledge of the bones and muscles no man can be sure of himself.

If he is lucky enough to get into some life class, and under a good master who is also an artist as well as a certificated drawing teacher, he will progress rapidly ; and also if he can occasionally at this period run over to Paris and spend an odd month in some of the modern artists' studios, he will have the more cause to congratulate his fortune. I urge this strongly even while I deplore that he has no opportunity of studying so directly under any of our own good men at home, who are either too modest or too busy to form schools as did the old masters.

CHAPTER VI

ON THE PASSIONS AND EXPRESSIONS OF THE HUMAN FIGURE

WE approach now that field where the novelist and the painter must both walk arm in arm, looking out upon humanity as studies in their different moods,—which the artist who stays in his studio painting from his model will never be able to catch. It is a gift of memory, and memory only, because the passions of men express themselves

H

and change more quickly than does an April sky. To acquire this knowledge you must go into all sorts of society, and amongst all conditions of men and women, without your note-book or colours; and what you witness you must store up in your memory, and reproduce when you return home as best you can.

Yet I may give you a few of the well-defined rules as they have been given to us by the old masters; for instance, love when satisfied will be expressed by the general placidity of the features, and the eyes which are self-engrossed. Love unsatisfied will be watchful and diffident; love suspicious is not a pretty sight, with its hanging jaws and contracted lids.

You have seen fear expressed in the staring eyes, wide open, and the half-open mouth, different in its glare from the wide-open eyes and parted mouth of wonder.

The hands also play their part in these passions, held up, but close to the body with palms showing, in the state of wonder; stretched out as if repulsing an enemy, but still open, in the state of fear; in passion they lie crossed easily; in anger they are clenched as if to strike.

In moments of anger or rage the face expresses itself differently according to the temperaments of the subject; yet the teeth are nearly always clenched and the lips compressed, with the brows drawn together, and the eye-balls shaded. In scorn the lips curl up and show the clenched teeth, while the frown still remains on the brow.

Anger and scorn are both pallid in colour, with perhaps a hectic spot on the cheek-bones ; rage grows scarlet ; pain is expressed in different contractions of the muscles ; and sleep is like death, calm and beautiful although not so bloodless.

CHAPTER VII

SOME ART TERMS

THERE are a few art terms which may perplex the beginner, and which I may as well explain here, to prevent any mistakes.

Aptitude, or *attitudine*, means the pose, posture, or action that a figure is capable of taking.

Cartoon is the design drawn and painted on different sheets of paper, pasted together for the future fresco.

Chiaroscuro is the light and shade of a picture.

Contour are the lines which make up a figure.

Feeling is the subtilty of colour or drawing expressed by the painter.

Manner, the style or characteristic of the artist.

Mezzo-relievo is when figures are represented raised up.

Palette, a flat piece of wood or china on which colours are spread, and held by the artist while working.

Tone, the scale or pitch, or degree of light and shadow, which a painter limits himself to in his work.

CHAPTER VIII

ON ETCHING

ETCHING is more decidedly the painter's mode of expressing himself in black and white than any of the other arts of engraving; and as in older times every painter of note amused himself when he could not use colours in this way, so, many of the modern men have of late years revived it; therefore it is needful in a painter's manual to give some brief directions as to how it should be done.

I suppose, by the time that the student takes up this art, he has practised for a considerable time with pen-and-ink drawings, so that he is not so much afraid to take up and use the etching needle.

For materials he will require :—

A few copper plates, small sizes.

A porcelain bath, such as photographers use, and large enough to hold the plate easily.

A ball of etching ground.

A dabber.

Etching needles of different sizes.

A dry point.

A scraper.

A burnisher.

An oil rubber.

Bottle of stopping-out varnish.

A shade for the eyes.

A bridge, or rest.

Bottle of turpentine or benzine.

Some wax tapers.

A bottle of nitrous or some other strong acid.

Whiting.

Washleather.

Charcoal sticks.

Tracing paper.

Blotting paper, white.

Crocus powder.

An oil-stone.

Some sheets of fine emery paper.

A small vice.

Some water-colour brushes.

And a good supply of soft white rags for wiping the plate in its various stages.

Etching is not what one might call a very cleanly amusement in any of its stages; the student must be prepared to dirty his fingers with the varnish and stain them with the acid. It also requires a good deal of patience and perseverance, but when mastered to an extent, it will be found well worth the trouble and smearing.

It must also be understood to be quite apart from all other kinds of engraving, therefore the student must never attempt to imitate the stiffness or closeness of either wood or steel engraving. He must strive to be free as if he were making a pencil or outline sketch, and try and put as much character into each line, and with as little labour as he possibly can get, i.e., he must try to be inspired by his subject and do his work with nervous spirit, if he desires to produce a good etching instead of a bad imitation of ordinary engraving.

Canaletto, the Venetian painter, and Seymour Haden are fair examples of what I mean for strong nervous lines in thin plates, for beginners to think upon and set before them as first and easy examples ; by and by they may learn to appreciate the subtilty and unmistakable work of Rembrandt and Whistler, but it is useless to set such intricate masters before them at the beginning.

When you have thoroughly cleaned your copper plate with whiting and water to remove all grease from it, hold it with your vice with the back towards a fire or over the gas until it is thoroughly warm, then take your ball of etching ground, which you have previously tied inside a silk bag, and rub it equally over the surface of the plate, until the ground has covered it equally over, for as it presses upon the heated plate it will melt and escape through the silk in sufficient quantity to coat over the copper. Be careful not to make the plate too hot, or it will spoil the quality of the ground coat.

After you have done this, dab it all equally over with your dabber, so as only to leave a very thin film of a clear golden colour.

When the ground has been all equally dabbed over, heat it again until it is once more melted, after which light a taper and hold it under the plate, surface downwards, with the flame just touching it ; this flame you pass over the plate rapidly until it is equally and thoroughly smoked, then set it aside to cool.

After it is perfectly cool, take a brush with some stopping-out varnish, and carefully coat over the back and edges of the plate so that the acid might not act upon them ; be particularly careful to cover all the copper except the face, which you have already covered with the etching ground. When this black varnish is dry, your plate is ready for your drawing.

On a sheet of paper the size of your copper,

you will now draw your design with pencil, and when ready rub the back of it with chalk, red or white as you like, and laying it down on the surface of the plate go over your outlines lightly with your pencil, which will so be traced through upon the etching ground ; remember that all you do must be reversed if you wish it to print correctly, therefore if it is a sketch from nature, a good plan is to look at it in a mirror, and draw it as you see it there.

You now take your etching needle and begin to use it as you would a pen on paper, only be sure to cut right through the ground and lay bare the copper without scratching its surface, particularly in the sky and distance ; the foreground may in some cases be all the better for a little scratching on those parts where you wish a strong heavy line, only with beginners it is best to leave that for the acid to do.

You are drawing a picture on a jet black ground with bright copper lines, so draw it as lightly and as closely as you can ; for when it is printed it will come out much more open and wide between the lines than it appears to be on the black plate. Be careful to make your lines as spidery and fine as you can, and also as free in their curves and twistings. Dust your plate as you go along with a soft camel or sable hair brush.

In the distance, where the lines are to be faint and little bitten, draw the lines as closely as you possibly can ; as you approach the foreground you can keep them a little more apart.

When your drawing is all complete, if you wish to take out any of the lines, you may paint them over with the stopping-out varnish, and scratch through that again as you desire.

You now mix your acid in your bath with water—you can test the strength required with a penny-piece ; drop it into the bath when mixed up, if it begins to bite it at once, i.e., cover it with little white froth-like bells, it is too strong, therefore reduce it with water, and *vice versâ* if it is too weak. The proper strength of the bath should be, if the penny lies for a moment or so without being touched, and then gradually begins to take on the bells.

For the distance it is best to have the bath weak ; you can always strengthen it as you get down to the foreground.

Do not inhale the fumes from the bath while you lean over the bath to watch the progress of the biting, and have ready beside you a basin of clear water to wash the plate when you take it out, also a feather to brush off the bubbles from the plate as it proceeds.

I cannot give you any time for the different

bitings, you must learn that from experience only, and by several failures at first; when you think it has been bitten long enough, take it out.

But to go back to the point when your drawing is done, and your plate is ready for the bath. Place it gently face upwards amongst the acid until it is completely covered, say half an inch over, then watch it carefully, brushing the frosted bells off as they appear and stirring the acid so that it may work freely. When you think the sky has been bitten deep enough, lift out your plate, wash it in the clear water and dry it thoroughly, after which paint over the sky carefully with the black stopping-varnish, and after that is dry, put it in once more amongst the acid.

After you think the distances are bitten sufficiently, remove the plate again, wash, dry, and stop it up to the middle distance, and so on for five or six times. An ordinary plate should require six different stages of biting and stopping before it is considered done; an elaborate plate perhaps twenty or even more.

When you consider that the plate is done, after washing and drying it take your rags and turpentine, and wash all the varnish carefully from it both back and front. It is now ready for the printer to take a first proof.

If you have a printing press, you may do this yourself, although you may find it more satisfactory to get it done for you. If you decide to do the printing yourself, this is the way to do it.

Get some etching or printer's ink, and after heating your plate, rub it over and well into the lines with your fingers, then go over it with a dabber until you are sure no line has been missed, after this wipe off all the superfluous ink from the surface, taking great care not to rub the ink out of the lines.

You then take some whiting upon the palm of your hand, and pass it deftly and lightly over the plate to give it a final polish, after which it is ready for the press.

Your proof paper is next damped thoroughly and placed, with your plate, the surface of which it covers, upon the travelling board or bed of the press, and over it several layers of flannel to keep it soft and make the paper press into the lines when under the roller, then turn the handle of your printing press, and the 'proof' is done.

Take care as you remove it from the plate, as it is apt to tear if not removed slowly and carefully.

When you have examined your first 'proof' you will find that you may have to go over some parts of your plate and re-etch it.

Therefore you must once more prepare your plate as at the beginning with your ground, only this time you do not 'smoke' the surface as at first, for you must be able to see your former lines. Lay the ground over carefully and varnish the back and edges, then make your corrections with your needle ; bite and stop out as before, and finally wash off with your turpentine and take another 'proof,' and so on, until you are satisfied that you can do no more with your plate, and that it is finished.

Some etchers, after they are satisfied that they can do no more with the acid, finish off their plate with a few touches of dry-point work, i.e., scratching or engraving the plate with thin graver or sharp-pointed steel tool ; but as this requires some experience and skill to do properly, the beginner had better not depend upon this. Do all that you can with the needle and acid until you have mastered these thoroughly.

The foregoing system is only one of many which etchers work in, but as it is the safest and easiest, I prefer to give it without perplexing you with any other.

In finally printing the plate many artistic effects are gained by leaving portions of the ink upon the plate, or by trailing some of the ink out of the lines with a soft muslin rag, and leaving it discretely about the edges ; this is called *retroussage*, and requires an artist to do it with proper effect. The old masters all printed their own plates, and so could make what effect they pleased, and as in painting, so in etching, every device is fair and legitimate if the result is satisfactory, so these artifices can only be discovered or created by the worker himself by experiment and many *failures*.

In working at a plate, the etcher, like the engraver, should sit in front of a window with a tissue-paper screen between him and the light ; he will use several steel needles, fine sharp ones for the distances, and blunter ones for the foreground.

The safest acid to use is nitrous, although nitric is more powerful ; the proportions of acid and water vary, but one part of acid to eight parts of water is a fair medium. Do not immerse your plate immediately after your acid is made up, not before the heat of its first mixing together has cooled. The baths may be of glass, vulcanite, or porcelain, but the latter is best.

The scraper is used for removing the burr, or furrow of the dry point, if required ; also to efface faulty lines. It ought to be kept in good condition, so as not to scratch the plate, and sharpened on the oil-stone with olive oil.

The burnisher is used to smooth down harsh

lines and accidental scratches on the plate ; great care must be taken to keep it bright and smooth, this is best done with olive oil and Tripoli powder.

When drawing on the plate it is best to keep some sheets of blotting-paper between your hand and the ground, that is, if you wish to dispense with the rest.

CHAPTER IX

ON ILLUSTRATIONS, AND THE USE OF DIFFERENT PROCESSES

IN illustrative work, the best drawings, of course, are those done for wood engravings or photogravure, as wash drawings. These may be made either in sepia, Indian ink, or with Chinese white and black, as the artist likes best to work. Formerly illustrators had to work on the wood block ; however, when I look back on these olden times, when we had to make our own drawings on the wood, and remember the agony we sometimes suffered when the engraving was done, and our own idea maltreated, I feel grateful to photography which saves all these pangs and acts as a check upon the engraver.

Now we make our sketch upon paper, which is reproduced upon the block, so that while the engraver works he has always the original before him to compare with his copy. Thus neither artist nor engraver can blame the other for faulty passages ; each must bear his own sins,—which is more satisfactory to all parties.

Pen-and-ink work is also greatly used now-a-days, and when used with type, if the compositor and artist act in concert, it harmonises best with half and quarter pages. A good pen-and-ink drawing should bear in its coarseness or fineness the exact proportion to the type used, i.e., a fine drawing should not have bold type near it, and *vice versâ* ; thus to have a perfectly harmonised book throughout, the printer should see the drawings which are to be inserted, or the artist see the type, and work accordingly. Perhaps in some cases this is not at present so much considered as it ought to be, and as it will yet be as illustrative art advances.

Therefore the student should be prepared to make strong lines as well as delicate work where wanted, and practise all styles if he wishes to become expert in this style of work.

There are several kinds of process paper prepared for artists to make work which may be more cheaply reproduced than wash drawings, and look more solid than pen and inks. They are none of them so satisfactory as wash drawings engraved ; yet, as they have often to be used, I give some specimens, and will also try to describe how they should be worked.

Fig. 8. Moonlight on the sea-coast, a specimen of white grained surface and pencil drawing. I have drawn this illustration entirely with an ordinary HB pencil, and leave it so, although it would have come out better if I had given it just a few

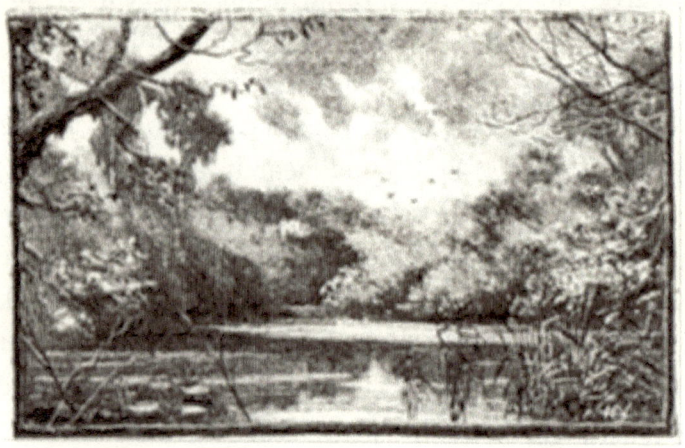

FIG. 15—A LAKE—SPECIMEN OF GRAINED-TINTED PROCESS-PAPER

sharp touches of pen-work ; however, as it is, it will give you the fairest idea of the capabilities of this paper.

It is bought all ready for drawing upon, and is not unlike ordinary lithographic transfer grained paper. To draw upon it properly you must go over it very lightly so as not to destroy the grain, and

fix your pencil drawing with fixature, it is thus
ready for the zincographer to do his work upon.

    Fig. 15. A lake. Specimen of *tinted*

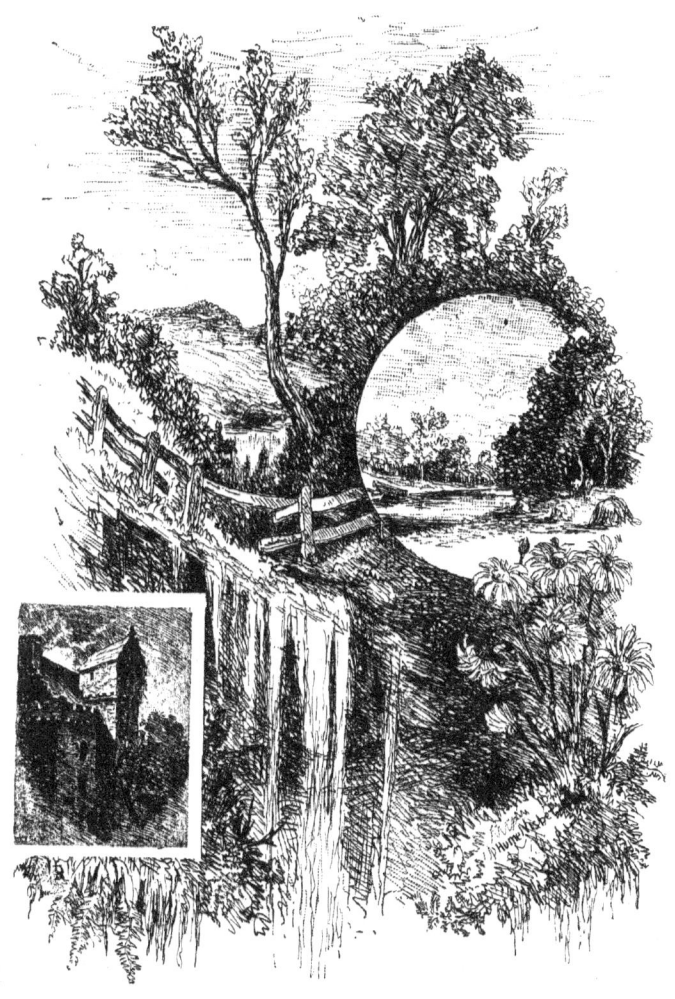

FIG. 16—COMBINATION SCENE—PROCESS AND PEN AND INK

grained or dotted process paper, with chalk drawing.

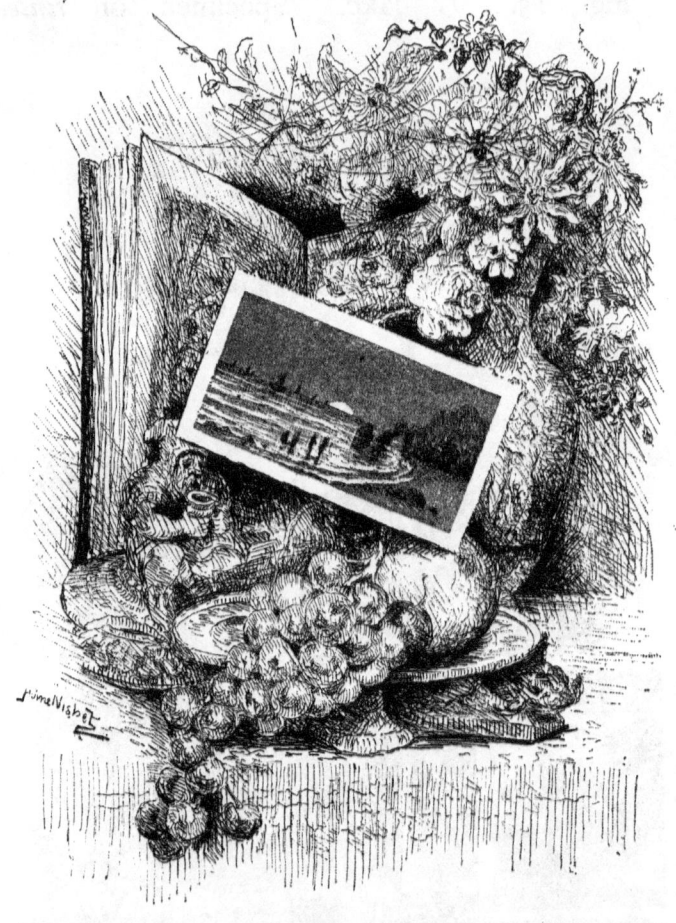

FIG. 17—FRUIT AND FLOWERS—COMBINATION OF PROCESS
AND PEN AND INK

This kind of paper is intended for scraping out
the lights and half-lights from; for this purpose

file-like scrapers are required, and knives of different
degrees of sharpness.   In this present drawing

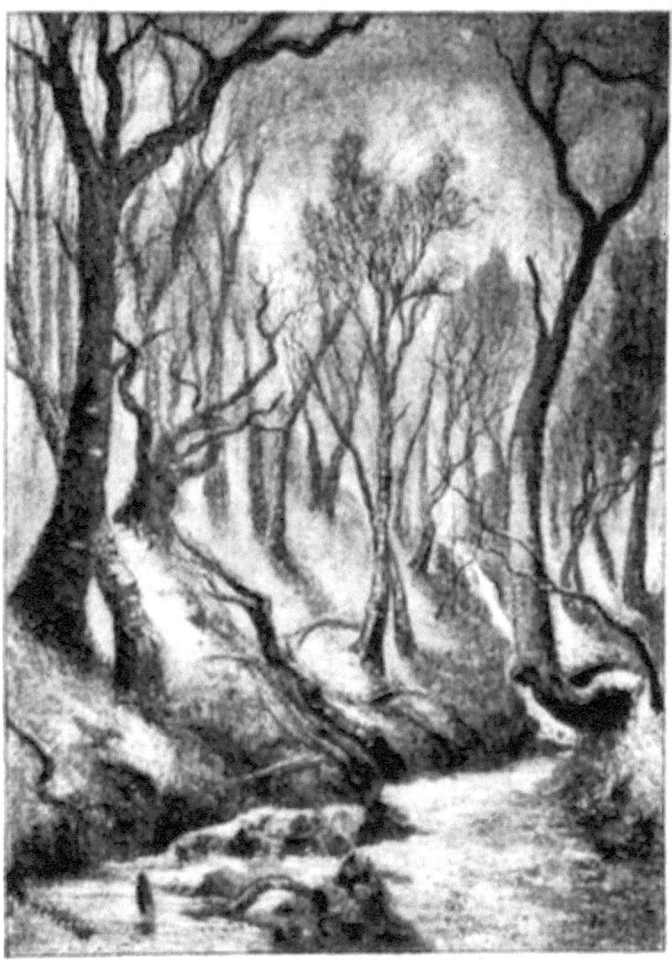

FIG. 18—SEPIA SKETCH—STUDY OF TREES

I have used lithographic chalk and Indian ink for
the finishing details,

Fig. 10. Twilight. Specimen of lined process tinted paper.

In this study I have done it throughout with

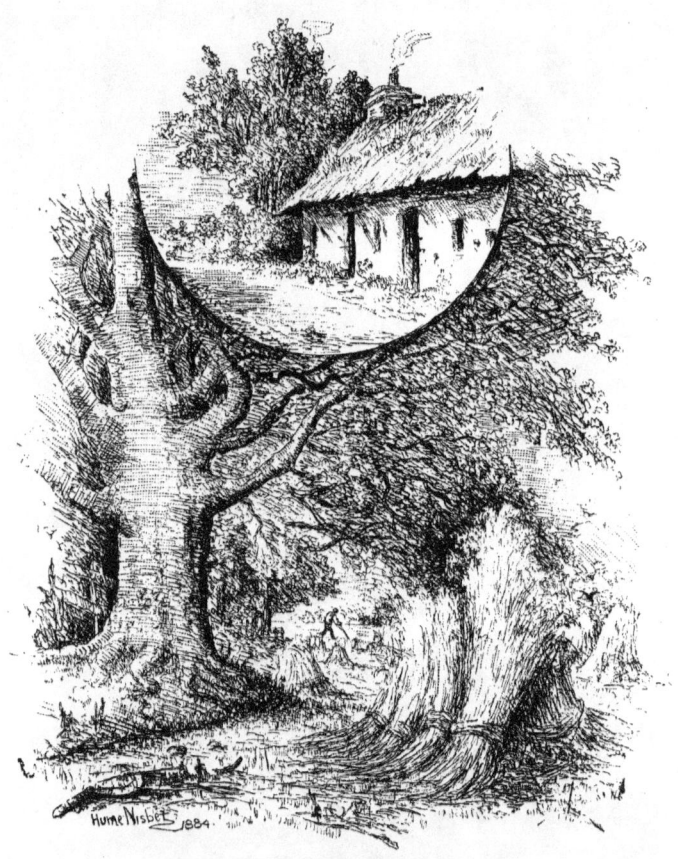

FIG. 19—STUDY IN PEN AND INK OF CORN-SHEAVES, BEECH-TREE, AND COTTAGE

pure pen-and-ink line-work, and as little scraping as possible; the sky is half-scraped, also parts of

the water ; the other portions are left in their
original state.

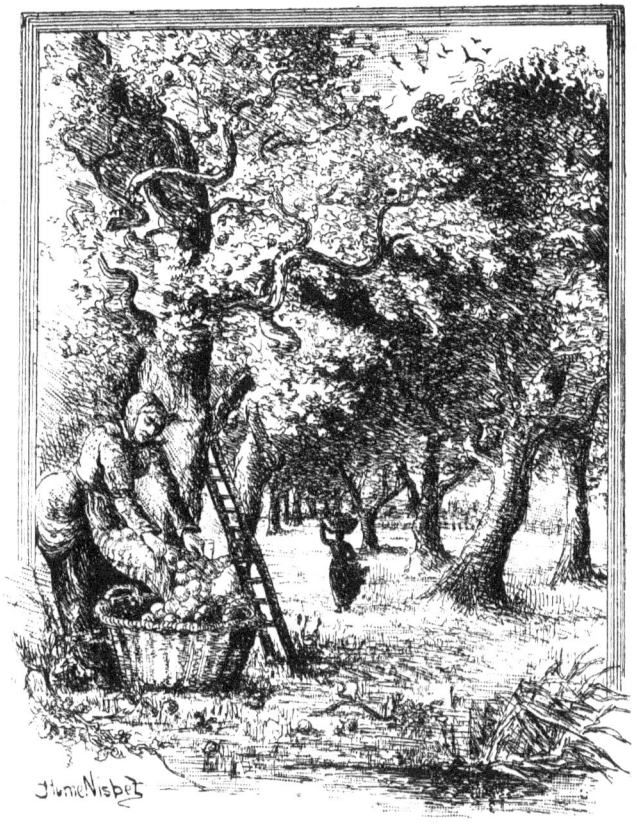

FIG. 20—STUDY IN PEN-ETCHING OF AN ORCHARD

Fig. 16. Combination scene.   Process paper
used along with pen-and-ink outlines.

Fig. 17. Study of fruit, flowers, and ornament,
with process line drawing.

These two studies are introduced to show how variety may be obtained in combination pages.

Fig. 18. Sepia sketch. Study of trees. This study is done originally in warm sepia, and reproduced by photographic process.

Frontispiece. The rising moon. Specimen of wood engraving.

Fig. 19. Study in pen and ink of corn, beech-tree, and cottage.

Fig. 20. Study in pen-etching of orchard.

I have now touched in a preliminary way upon all the different modes connected most directly with art, and may leave the student at this point to practise for himself. When he gets far enough advanced, I would recommend to his notice my 'Life and Nature Studies,' which were designed and written expressly for artists, who may find themselves the better for hints on inspiration as well as those dry measurements of anatomy, and ships, &c., with composition, artistic botany and geology, also some of those ethical ideas which nature and art can suggest to the poetic and imaginative mind. To that work I must refer you if you desire to advance farther than this present manual can carry you.

CONCLUDING REMARKS

Never be in a hurry over your work, and always have your drawing perfect as you proceed.

When you come to colour, think upon that only, before you begin your subject ; you must already be satisfied with your proportions and out-lines. Leave no harsh or over-prominent lines or edges, for your picture is only finished when each part fits into the other, and no part unduly obtrudes or claims undue attention, for this is the perfection of harmony. When the story is told smoothly and with quiet effect, the eye should be led up gradu-ally to the principal portion, not drawn towards it with a jerk.

Keep your box, colours, brushes, and materials always tidy and clean, and your mind always free from haste or feverish anxieties.

So you will glide through the different stages, enjoying your work, and, when it is finished, the onlookers will also be satisfied with the result.

Lastly, I would give you the advice of that great French philosopher and poet, Victor Hugo, who did so much true work himself. In all your work :—

Try to be wise, meek, good, with anxious care,
Nor take one step which is not propt by prayer.